UNLOCK THEIR FUTURE

A Skills-based approach to teaching and learning English

Edited by

VINEY KIRPAL
(Former Professor of English, IIT Bombay)

and

SHRIDHAR B. GOKHALE
(Former Professor, Department of English,
Pune University)

Sterling Paperbacks

STERLING PAPERBACKS
An imprint of
Sterling Publishers (P) Ltd.
A-59, Okhla Industrial Area, Phase-II, New Delhi-110020
Tel: 26387070, 26386209; Fax: 91-11-26383788
E-mail: mail@sterlingpublishers.com
www.sterlingpublishers.com

Unlock their Future
A Skills-based approach to teaching and learning English
© 2011, *Viney Kirpal and Shridhar B. Gokhale*
ISBN 978 81 207 6139 1

All rights are reserved.
No part of this publication may be reproduced, stored in a retrieval system or transmitted, in any form or by any means, mechanical, photocopying, recording or otherwise, without prior written permission of the author.

Printed in India

Printed and Published by Sterling Publishers Pvt. Ltd., New Delhi-110 020.

"India takes pride in having the youngest population in the world, which it expects will make the country the most advanced in the world by 2020.

But, this demographic advantage will become a liability if we fail to address the fundamental issue of creating committed teachers to convert this huge human resource into a skilled manpower to drive the engine of the growth."

Dr. R M Mashelkar
Director General, CSIR

Acknowledgements

A book is made by many people. Most gratefully and humbly we acknowledge the help of all the following friends, associates and well wishers:

- All the teachers at the workshop 'How to Teach English Language' held in Pune in January 2007
- Professor Ashok Kelkar, our former teacher
- Dr. Shridhar Shukla, Managing Director, GS LAB, Pune and good friend
- Ms. Jaslene Bawa, another friend
- Ms. Sheelam Bawa, former Admin. Officer Global Institute of Integrated Training, Pune
- Ms. Archana Kavade, former Office Assistant, GREAT Foundation, Pune
- Ms. Gulfam Shaikh, Office Assistant, GREAT Foundation, Pune
- Ms. Aishwarya Gore, Office Assistant, Global Institute of Integrated Training, Pune
- Ms. Vinny Paul, Office Assistant, Department of English, Pune University
- Mr. S. K. Ghai, Managing Director and his team, Sterling Publishers, New Delhi.

Viney Kirpal
Shridhar B. Gokhale

Contents

	Acknowledgements	iv
1.	Introduction *Viney Kirpal and Shridhar B. Gokhale*	1

Spoken English

2.	Some Remarks on the Teaching of Spoken English and Conversational English *Shridhar B. Gokhale*	12
3.	How Much English Speech Does a Teacher Need? Teaching Spoken English and the Indian Teacher *Sudhakar Marathe*	17
4.	Computer Assisted Language Learning *T. Ravichandran*	43

Writing Skills

5.	Everything is an Argument: A Thematic Approach to Teaching the English Course *Sharmita Lahiri*	54
6.	How I Teach Paragraph and Essay Writing *Viney Kirpal*	62

Reading Skills

7.	Teaching Prose *Prabha Sampath*	76
8.	Reading Better and Faster *Viney Kirpal*	84
9.	Note Taking Skills *Niloufer Aga*	94

Grammar and Word Power Development

10.	Teaching of Grammar *Shridhar B. Gokhale*	108
11.	Teaching of Grammar and Vocabulary *Simon G. Bernabas*	114
12.	Enriching Vocabulary *Shirin Shaikh*	129
13.	Teaching Language to Large Classes *Madhuri Gokhale*	144
14.	Using a Dictionary *Shridhar B. Gokhale*	152
15.	Remedial English: A Case Study *Viney Kirpal*	157
16.	The Testing of Language Skills *Shridhar B. Gokhale*	167

English for Professional Purposes

17.	Writing Emails *Viney Kirpal*	172
18.	English for Specific Purposes *Grace Jacob*	186

1 Introduction
Viney Kirpal and Shridhar B. Gokhale

Teaching and learning are indivisible sides of the same coin. The present scene of the teaching and learning of English in India is in a mess. Indeed, there is too much of *teaching* of English in India, beginning with Std. I in some states, and Std. V in others, and continuing till graduation. In comparison, the learning of English, seems almost negligible.

Performance in Examinations v/s Performance in Jobs

This narrative of failure is often masked by the performance of students in school and university examinations. While a good number of students 'manage' to fare well in tests and examinations, most graduates are unable to express themselves in English when applying for a job or facing a job interview. Typically, our graduates cannot comprehend a news broadcast on the radio or television, cannot talk about their strengths or weaknesses. They feel diffident about participating in a group discussion or reading in English and whenever they do, they do so slowly and painfully. They cannot write an effective curriculum vitae! The depressing realisation is that there are lakhs of teachers involved in the teaching of English from primary school to university levels but the teaching of English has resulted in little learning. This story of national waste of time, money and energy has been going on for the last 60 years.

Ideally, not more than three years is required to acquire a reasonable amount of mastery over a language. This is ably proved by reputed institutes teaching French or German in India. English is taught for 15 long years in India and examinations are passed fairly successfully. Yet students seem unable to cope with the reasonable demands of the job market. Obviously, English is being taught in India more from the examination point of view than as a preparation for tangible life skills.

To cover up for their lack of success, teachers often play the 'blame-game'. University teachers blame college teachers, college teachers blame school teachers, school teachers blame parents – and so the story goes on. The question is: whose responsibility is it to help students master English? Perhaps the solution to these problems lies not in the quantitative expansion of the teaching of English, but rather in its qualitative enrichment. Do teachers have no option but to perpetuate the history of non-success in teaching students English? Or is it possible to bring about positive changes in this situation slowly and steadily?

The present book has its genesis in the conviction that it is possible *and* desirable to introduce modifications in the current scene of teaching English in India. Indeed each one of us, teachers and students of English, can contribute to make it more interesting and relevant and participate in the process of its transformation. To do so requires that we first understand some of the factors which work against the goal of learning English.

Factors which Obstruct the Learning of English

Many factors seem to work against this objective. First, our students appear to understand the importance of possessing language skills only after graduation when they need to face interviews to find placement or to go abroad for higher studies. Then they enrol for exorbitantly-priced private classes that may help them sail through job interviews or clear English tests that entitle them to study abroad. We cannot say if the teachers of these crash courses are more skilled language teachers than those in the colleges. What we can be sure of is that our students are more motivated to learn English out of college than when it is being taught so readily and inexpensively in our schools and colleges.

Partly this is so because passing the compulsory English course in Indian Universities is ridiculously easy. The pass mark is a low 35 per cent most times even though students have been exposed to similar courses in English at school and college. No wonder our students have acquired the art of getting through the examination without knowing English. Their teachers also seem to collude with them by teaching them only the 'techniques' of passing the examination. Further, the university examination is not aimed at testing particular language skills. Compare it with the SAT or TOEFL tests and you will observe the seriousness with which students approach them because these tests evaluate specific skills and set high standards of passing. Frankly speaking, the purpose of college English courses and the examination system is just not clear.

Secondly, the typical language course is syllabus-driven. Teaching designed to complete the syllabus is unfortunately marks-directed and not competencies-oriented. In the current day professional world which our students join after graduation, the emphasis is on skills and competencies, and not on scores or syllabi. An employee who has to make presentations must show he knows how to organize his matter in a logical and lively manner. They must be able to support it with data and documents and present it with power point slides. One who has to write or speak with customers must know how to understand their communication and respond with correct grammar, apt vocabulary, and appropriate and courteous use of language. In this world, skills, and not grades or mark lists count.

The effect on business of employees not knowing how to speak or write grammatically correct sentences, can prove very costly to the company. Today employees are expected to communicate globally. They are expected to understand customer requirements as well as to know how to put across their ideas lucidly. No company would like to lose customers because of poor communication on the part of their employees. It would rather ask such an associate to leave if she or he did not improve within a reasonable timeframe.

Again, the college curriculum does not reflect the demands on students in terms of the terminal linguistic behaviour expected in the 21st century. The curriculum contains a statement of aims and objectives of a

Anachronistic College Curricula

particular course but these are not directly linked with what students are expected to be able to do either in higher studies or in their jobs. Some curricula do mention specific language skills that students are expected to master but there is often no connection between the stated aims and objectives and the other components of the curriculum, viz the syllabus and the textbook, the teaching methodology and the examinations. The syllabus is often content-based and not skills-based and the textbook is usually a collection of prose or verse passages mainly from literature. The textbook may contain passages from the 18 or 19th century that are on topics which are of little interest to students. We are quite sure that students today would love to study passages relating to films, gaming, advertising, fashions, sports, recent scientific discoveries, new age lifestyles, the generation next mindset etc. But such topics are conspicuous by their absence. In order to ascertain effective teaching or learning it is necessary that students 'enjoy' what they study. This is ignored while formulating the syllabus or selecting the textbook.

Obviously students are not able to master contemporary English if they are exposed to obsolete forms of English styles.

The teacher, however, often believes that his duty is to 'finish' the topics or 'cover' the syllabus and that this is done effectively by *teaching* the textbook. The textbook is, in fact, only an excuse for teaching English. Many teachers attach too much value to the content of the textbook and ignore the skills which are supposed to be developed through the content. Resourceful teachers use other supplementary materials from different sources and focus on the language skills rather than on the content of the textbook. Teachers need to use sources like news reports, TV interviews, business speak, popular songs, advertisements, jokes and computer assisted language learning programmes such as You Tube videos and other online lessons in addition to the textbook to expose students to 'living' English and enhance the interest value of their studies.

This is easier said than done. As stated earlier, a teacher of English has to face a large number of problems

- the inconsistent, half-hearted and unrealistic policies about the teaching of English, the love-hate attitude to the language, the anachronistic syllabi and textbook, the unmitigated use of 'lecturing' as the only technique of teaching, unmotivated and bored learners, overcrowded and heterogeneous classes, the non-possession of textbooks by a majority of students and the indifferent examination system that we have already hinted at earlier.

To overcome some of these problems, most teachers of English teach English through the regional language or Hindi, the national language. No one would oppose the use of Indian languages in compulsory English classes for limited purposes, in emergencies or in difficult situations but this should be restricted to the minimum. In most situations, a teacher of English must be able to teach English 'through' English. This is valuable because then the students get a better and longer exposure to the use of English. A teacher should be able to use simple English in the classroom—so simple that it is comprehended even by weak students. It is well-known that speaking 'simple' English is one of the most difficult tasks but a teacher of English must strive hard to develop this ability. Unfortunately, many teachers appear to be comfortable with the situation. They give excuses to rationalize the state of English teaching today. Their sense of complacency comes from the fact that they can have an easier time complying with the system than going beyond it.

How Teachers 'Overcome' Problems

The fact of mixed English proficiency levels can also affect the motivation of both students and teachers. Good students do not want to come to a class which focuses on explaining extracts and essays that they can understand in one reading. The average and weak students want the teacher to explain everything so that they can get through the examination. Besides comprising mixed linguistic ability students, college classes are also made up of students belonging to different socio-economic groups. The correlation between their social strata and the kind of schools they have studied in, is apparent. Rich students, generally speaking, study in good English schools which give them a sound linguistic foundation. The less privileged are comparatively not so well-prepared by their schools. The dilemma for the teacher is: How should she interest all her students through appropriate language activities? How should she develop her students' language skills to the level where they can work with fair amount of independence?

Furthermore, the challenges of teaching English in India are rooted not only in the class composition and a prescribed textbook, but also in the lack of autonomy and alternative teaching methods available to teachers. 'Lecturing' is the sole technique used by most teachers in their classes. It is sometimes thought that the teacher's job is to read the text aloud, explain it, discuss its important aspects and dictate answers to comprehension questions while the student's job is to listen to her and take down notes. What we may not realize is that this type of teaching reduces the students into passive recipients. Most of our classes are teacher-centric and unless we turn them into learner-centric interactions, the 'learning' of English may never take place. There must be greater and more lively exchanges between teachers and students and the classes should involve more activities on the part of students. It is not being suggested here that a teacher of English must never lecture. Rather, she or he should use lecturing judiciously and only for a part of the total class time because lecturing makes it harder to assess whether or not the students have learnt the language skills.

Choosing the Right Teaching Materials and Methods

Majority of the teachers are unable to choose the language teaching materials appropriate to the needs of their students. Dissatisfaction with the prescribed textbook is almost universal and possibly a reason for de-motivation among teachers. You would agree that no textbook can meet the entire set of requirements of all the students in the class. Every textbook seems to have been designed for an imaginary group of students whose exact replica may never be found in the actual classroom. So, perhaps it is unrealistic to expect a perfect textbook. Prodromou (1992) has observed that dissatisfaction with the textbook may arise out of an "illusion that pre-fabricated solutions do exist for what are actually human problems" (142). He suggests, instead, that we see the textbook "as a resource and a 'holding structure' through and within which creative lessons happened" (143). Prodromou's remark is important for the direction in which English teachers could go. Dependence on the course textbook can lead to ill-prepared, mechanical teaching. Instead, the teacher must push the limits of any given textbook and complement it with his or her skill and choice of selections.

Undoubtedly, timely completion of the syllabus is the duty of every teacher. However, teachers have also to possess the art of selecting parts to emphasize or de-emphasize in their teaching after they have estimated, at the outset, the real life needs of their students. This is where our students may be made to feel excited with the material and the innovative teaching methods that a teacher brings to the class. This is also the point where teachers can feel satisfied and deliver results. But few teachers seem inclined to put in the extra effort this calls for.

Our contributors are making a similar point: They urge teachers to be creative and imaginative and to empower their students in the essential linguistic skills through the language course. Teachers could devise a variety of activities and exercises, and use methods which would help their students benefit from the most. Surely, all of us want to make the classroom an interesting and student-oriented place. If we make it theoretical and mechanical, it will not succeed because our students are adults. Instead, we can emphasize the practical aspects of language in use. For example, getting our students to read faster and with depth, write effectively, speak with confidence, and listen in ways that will make them perceive the difference in their own linguistic capabilities could work wonders. So, we need to make our classes interactive and give students the opportunity to *use* the language. Let us encourage them to think about the language whether we are teaching them the pure language skills or language as literature. Let us allow them to express themselves freely and experience the confidence and joy of using the language elegantly. They will be expected to use English effectively in the workplace, a few years hence, so why not make the classroom their training ground.

The teacher of a course is the soul of a class. He or she can breathe life into it or stifle it. With this knowledge, let us exert ourselves to make the English course useful to students so that they feel that their time has been well-spent. Every student who attends our class must feel that he or she has learnt to speak, write, listen, read, understand and think a little better in English than when they started. Give them the tools to succeed with the acquisition of language skills, give them regular practice and then see for ourselves the confidence with which they use English. Lastly praise, so lacking in our classrooms, if given as positive reinforcement, would act as a much-needed tonic to motivate all our students to learn.

Teachers Must Set an Example

To achieve this, teachers must set an example. Be good practitioners of language who can write well, speak fluently and correctly, be efficient readers and makers of notes, careful listeners and thought-generating individuals. Ironically, many an English teacher speaks and teaches incorrect English and is not even aware of the damage he or she does to the students day after day. Quite a few also do not know or do not want to know that they are bad and boring teachers. They blame the students for lacking seriousness and do little to train themselves in the latest teaching methods that would make their classes more stimulating.

In order to improve our own competence and proficiency in English teaching, it is desirable that we participate in in-service teacher training courses offered by reputed institutions. The onus of attracting students to our classes lies on us. It is also our responsibility to update our knowledge of the English language and fluency in its use. In this context, the editors of the present book believe that the process of change can begin with teacher-empowerment, teacher-enrichment and re-orientation of the examination system. A paradigm shift on the part of English teachers, Boards of Studies and universities, along with inputs from experienced educationists, industrialists and corporate heads, can alter the current scene of teaching and learning English for ever.[1]

Finally, as Von Humboldt (1974) has observed that teachers cannot really teach language, they can only create conditions in which it will develop spontaneously in the mind. He adds that this must be preceded, by a constant attempt to understand the learning process a lot better. The exact moment when a student learns to use language competently is not too well-known. We also do not know how the shift from unconscious incompetence to conscious incompetence to conscious/unconscious competence happens. However, it is when a teacher realises that her job is to help her students make this progressive shift she has already taken the first step towards their acquiring it.

Given the complex historical, political, socio-economic and cultural context in which it is taught, English is a difficult language to teach. For all said and done, it is a second, or even third language for most Indians. It is generally learnt from grammar books and English "digests" or guide books. However, the importance of English is growing with the changed business scene where a student from a small town and a metro have to equally face the challenge of using English with English -speaking foreign customers and business clients. Therefore, the language that is decried publicly and desired privately can no longer be treated as a low status language. Teachers of English must see it as a high status language and teach it more effectively. That would motivate both the teacher and the taught to engage with the study of language more seriously.

Why this Volume?

You may want to know why we have compiled this volume on the teaching of English and how it is different from other books on the teaching of English. Our answer follows. Most books are theoretical in nature whereas this book has adopted a very practical skills-based approach. So practical are its contents that even a student can teach himself or herself the language skill they want to learn. Each of the contributors is an experienced teacher and has faced similar difficulties as other teachers face every day. Contributors were requested to write about the practices, methods and activities they have successfully used in their English language classes and they have been generous enough to do so.

Unlock their Future represents team reflection on the important subject of teaching English in the Indian classroom today. Twenty-first century students, as we all can observe, are more focused and career-oriented than any earlier generation. They are more computer savvy, net savvy and better informed than their teachers would like to credit them with. Students today are more intelligent, alert and demanding than ever before. They respond less to dull, bookish instruction than to stimulating, learner-centred, activities-oriented classroom engagement. Therefore, no matter what the constraints—the syllabus, the time allotted, the university examination pattern, de-motivated students —the onus of turning pupils into skilful users of English lies only with one person, namely their teacher. Let us remember that that teacher is none other than each one of us!

Note

1. As this manuscript was about to go to press, one read the heartening news report that the Maharashtra State Higher Education Department is planning to revise the arts, commerce and science syllabi with emphasis on practical skills from June 2010. According to the news report, a meeting of the Directors of Boards of College and University Development, Deans and Chairmen of the Board of Studies was convened by Mr. R. V. Keerdak, Director, Higher Education where he said, "The syllabi of arts, science and commerce are becoming irrelevant as they have no connection to the present scenario. The department is keen on making it relevant [by making it more skills-based]."

'Skill-based uniform syllabi across varsities to meet the demands of the times' in Pune Newsline, *The Indian Express*, 15th March 2010.

References

1. Corder, S.P. (1974). Summarizes Von Humboldt's observations in 'The significance of learner's errors' in Richards, J. *Error Analysis: Perspectives on Second Language Acquisition.* London: Longman:19-27.
2. Prodromou, L.(1992), *Mixed Ability Classes*. London: Macmillan Publishers Ltd.

Spoken English

2. Some Remarks on the Teaching of Spoken English and Conversational English

Shridhar B. Gokhale

Introduction

Globalization and internationalization have raised the demand for effective Spoken English and Conversational English. The ability to make presentations has gained significantly in importance. The ever-increasing number of coaching classes in Spoken English testify to this trend.

The term 'Spoken English' as used in this article refers to pronunciation and accent in general. It involves the correct articulation of vowel and consonant sounds, and correct accentual, rhythmic and intonational patterns. The term 'Conversational English' is used in this article to refer to the ability to participate orally in different situations and involves interacting with one or more persons including pubic speaking. The two terms are seen as complementary to each other and competence in one of them may lead to competence in the other.

The Model for Pronunciation

There are a number of varieties of English all over the world and British English, American English, Australian English, Canadian English etc. are standard varieties of English. The teaching model in India has conventionally been Standard British English. Even if teachers of English in India attempt to teach British English, at best they can teach some variety of Indian English. It is impossible and even undesirable to try to teach British English as the model of pronunciation in India, because most teachers have not mastered it. It is not possible for teachers to teach something that they have not mastered. The only practical solution to the problem is that we should agree to teach GIE, i.e. General Indian English, proposed by Bansal and Harrison proposed by Bansal and Harrison (1994) as the model of pronunciation. Teachers can project it with greater confidence and students can learn it more successfully and therefore, both teachers and students experience a greater sense of satisfaction. We do not need to blindly imitate the model of British R. P. Another advantage in following GIE as a model is that our accent would sound natural and not artificial.

Building Up Confidence Among Students

Confidence is probably the first step to success in Spoken English and Conversational English. Most students are afraid of speaking English, because they believe that they would make errors the moment they opened their mouths. However, it must be understood clearly that errors are the strategies of learning and one masters any skill only by making mistakes. I believe that the best teacher is he or she who gives maximum opportunities to students of making mistakes. The teacher needs to create an atmosphere in the class, which convinces students that nothing terrible would happen if they made mistakes. The teacher should convince himself/herself first and then students that fluency is more important in communication than accuracy and that if communication takes place effectively, grammatical correctness is a secondary factor.

The Concept of Fluency

Everyone aims at being a fluent speaker of a language. However, the concept of fluency is often misunderstood within India. It is often equated with fast speech. The term 'fluency' is related to the word 'flow' and anything that flows smoothly is fluent. There is no harm in speaking slowly. It is important to follow our natural speed. Of course, in order to be a fluent speaker, we must avoid hesitation, long pauses or what are sometimes described as voiced pauses (...er...). One of the factors contributing to fluency is more efficient mental planning.

Procedure for Teaching: How to Speak in Different Situations?

Conversational English often includes topics like 'Thanking People', 'Introducing Others', 'Agreement and Disagreement' and 'Making Inquiries'. Each topic involves two or more speakers. A lot of print and audio material is available on Conversational English and there are many simple but useful techniques of teaching it.

These materials provide dialogues that students may be initially asked to read silently or listen to. That would acquaint them with the situation. The next step is to assign different roles to students and ask them to read their parts effectively. At this stage, students need to be trained in effective reading of dialogues. After a few repetitions, students could be encouraged to remember the dialogues and say them aloud without referring to the printed text. At this stage, students are not expected to learn the dialogues by heart, but they are expected to remember the content and express it in their own language. This is a good opportunity for students to practise their linguistic skills. My experience suggests that in such cases students sometimes change the content and this is very welcome. The dialogue may proceed in an unforeseen direction and both the students should be able to interact appropriately in the new situation.

The next step is to be independent of the printed text. Students can be assigned their roles and the situation can be explained to them. Students have greater freedom here and they are required to be more imaginative and resourceful. However, sometimes it is noticed that one of the students does not speak much and therefore, the conversation reaches a dead end! This can be easily avoided if the teacher plays one of the roles in the conversation. The teacher can give a proper direction to the conversation and extend it, if necessary. In such a situation, the teacher can make even a reticent student speak more by asking him questions. This will finally lead to a more extended conversation on the part of students.

Procedure for Teaching Public Speaking

Planning and organization play an important role in a successful oral presentation or public speaking. Students should be encouraged to think in terms of three or four points and their sub-points before beginning any presentation and note them down on a piece of paper. It is perfectly all right to refer to these points from time to time while speaking. At a more advanced stage, a student may keep the paper in his pocket or may not need to write points on it, because he would have done mental planning.

Eye contact is of vital importance in public speaking and plays a significant role in making a speaker confident. Eye contact consists in looking almost at each member of the audience at least for some time. Some speakers look at the floor or the ceiling or out of the window all the time. Looking at the audience and having good eye contact provides the speaker with valuable feedback about the interest, motivation and comprehension of the audience.

In order to encourage students to practice public speaking effectively, it is necessary to choose a topic that would interest all the students and be within the range of their experience and linguistic competence. With weaker students, one of the early topics can be 'Self-Introduction'. It is important to see to it that there is some element of novelty or creativity in every task that students are assigned. In my workshops, I make them aware of the fact through examples that each one of us is extraordinary in some sense and that each one is different from the others in some respect. I give them time to think about the feature which distinguishes them from all the others. While introducing themselves, I ask students to begin by giving routine details like name, profession and background and then talk about one of their own special features like sportsmanship, punctuality and love of music. While talking about the latter, I ask them to explain the feature, give experiences related to that from their own lives and say how they feel about the particular feature. The advantage in making students do this is that there is something new and unexpected in each student's presentation and the class enjoys such presentations. After each presentation, I ask them to specify both the strong points and weak points of each speaker. I add my own comments. I compliment each student for good points of his presentation and help him/her overcome the weaknesses by giving them practical training or advice. My experience indicates that all this boosts up students' self-confidence and considerably improves their performance.

In the procedure outlined above, I treat each student as a unique human being and try to bring out the best from even an average student.

Concluding Remarks

An effective conversationalist pays attention to both the aspects — what to say and how to say it. Qualities like thoughtfulness, originality and sincerity play a crucial role in deciding what to say. However, the focus of the article has been on how to say something. The practical suggestions made above are intended to make teachers more effective instructors and to make learners more successful practitioners of Spoken English and Conversational English.

Reference

Bansal, R. K. and Harrison, J. B (1994). *Spoken English*, Hyderabad: Orient Longman.

3

How Much English Speech Does a Teacher Need? Teaching Spoken English and the Indian Teacher

*Sudhakar Marathe**

The proof of the pudding is in the eating.

> Television News, 28 July 2008: Many highly qualified young people in Kerala are jobless because they speak English poorly and with a heavy Malayali accent.

This chapter is deliberately titled after a tale of Count Leo Tolstoy: land is offered to poor people; each man can have as much land as he can perambulate in the course of a day from sunrise to sunset. One man, most awfully greedy, literally walks himself to death, falling down at the point of return at sunset. *Then* all the land he needs is a hole in the ground that is 6 feet by 3! The moral of the story: Greed comes to grief.

However, if the Old Count were to write about English teachers, he would write with the opposite ending, endorsing, not condemning 'greed' or aspiration to command as *much* speech as possible, *not* wanting as little as possible. The greedier the teacher the better he can teach. That, indeed, is the key to learning, enhancing and teaching the fundamental skills in a language, listening and speaking. Reading and writing *are* secondary skills. Where speech is concerned the more a

---

*Sudhakar Marathe Ph.D. is former Professor of English and Dean, School of Humanities at the University of Hyderabad. Earlier, he did his M.A. from Pune University as well as taught Phonetics at the Department of English, Pune University. He has written seven books on language, literature and translated works.

teacher commands the better, and the better he speaks, the better he will teach anything. No language teacher does his duty unless he teaches these two skills as fully and holistically as possible, not poorly, not partially, not weakly, not superficially. In speech the rule is very simple, indeed: what you cannot do, you cannot teach: The proof of the pudding is in the eating.

Let us first consider the present situation in English teaching in India. Virtually no teacher is even moderately competent in speech. Yet we all speak for **90%** of the time in class. Most are unaware of the power one acquires from speaking any language well. Indeed, dismiss the misconception from your minds that we are allocating some special status to English. The argument of this chapter applies equally to any language we learn, including a second language such as Hindi or Kannada. Other teachers employ an ostrich-like or escapist argument: why must we learn to speak English well? In fact the real question is why *not* learn to speak English well? And more and more teachers accept the meaningless argument that "communication is enough", without knowing what communication means. Therefore, they deprive their students of genuine power of communication. Very simply, what is worth doing is worth doing well. And, equally simply, today *every* student desires to learn effective English speech. It is our *basic* job to teach what they need and want.

In speech words and grammar mean very little without their rendering in speech. Speech consecrates words and grammar, gives them their meaning in context, interprets them according to speaker, listener and the circumstances in which one communicates. It allows one to make more meaning than words and grammar can ever make by verbally fitting language into context. Literally, a teacher *is* what he *says*. That is why in general one must consider the following items to ensure that our teaching of speech is correct and effective and *powerful* in communication:

- Basic Notions about Speech & Speech-&-Writing
- Misconceptions about Speech
- Teacher as Model: Service & Disservice

- From Single Words to Grammar to Style to Literature
- The Basics of Speech
- The Basics of English Speech
- English Vowels and Consonants
- Basic English Stress and Rhythm
- Basic English Stress, Rhythm and Intonation
- Speech as Real-Life Drama
- Speech Models for Teachers and for Students
- Preventing and Avoiding Common Errors.

It is impossible to ignore the fact that for almost all students in India their English teacher is still the only model of speech. That is a very grave and responsible situation. It means that a teacher makes or mars his students' English speech. His job is simple and unambiguous: (1) provide exposure to good speech and (2) enable students to speak well. The first key for teachers is providing *EXPOSURE TO CORRECT AND EFFECTIVE SPOKEN ENGLISH*; the second key is *ENABLING students* so that they can manage anything they may meet in English outside school or college:

The greater the exposure, the more students learn;
The richer the exposure, the more effective the language students learn;
The more varied exposure, the better students learn;
The more fluent the exposure, the more fluent students become;
The more flexible the exposure, the more flexible students become;
The more confident the exposure, the more confident students become;
The more appropriate the exposure, the more appropriate your students' speech.

This exposure comes from the same (re-)source—the PASSIVE and ACTIVE English the teacher ACTUALLY POSSESSES:

The more he can *do* the more effective the language he takes into class;
The more effective language he takes into class, the more language he uses;

The more language he uses, the greater the chance for students to learn;
The better the language he uses, the better he becomes as a model.

Let us start with an obvious yet far from simple example. One knows one must say "Good morning" or "Good morning, children" or "Good morning, class". But is that all? And isn't it boring to keep saying it every day? And isn't it seriously limiting for language learning to say the same thing **180** days in the year without variation appropriate to situation and individual? Consider the following—

1. "Good morning, Class."

   When and how to say this? Routinely? In a friendly manner, cheerfully, encouragingly? How does one do that?

2. "Good morning, children / students."

   When and how to say this? Routinely? In a friendly manner, cheerfully, encouragingly? How does one do that?

3. "Good morning, everyone."

   When and how to say this? Routinely? In a friendly manner, cheerfully, encouragingly? How does one do that?

4. "Good morning to you."

   When and how to say this? Routinely? In a friendly manner, cheerfully, encouragingly? How does one do that?

5. "Good morning to you all."

   When and how to say this? Routinely? In a friendly manner, cheerfully, encouragingly? How does one do that?

6. "Good morning, Suresh."

   When and how to say this? Routinely? In a friendly manner, cheerfully, encouragingly? How does one do that?

7. "Good morning, dear."

   When and how to say this? Routinely? In a friendly manner, cheerfully, encouragingly? How does one do that?

8. "Good morning, my dear."
   When and how to say this? Routinely? In a friendly manner, cheerfully, encouragingly? How does one do that?
9. "Not a very good morning, is it? It's hot already!"
   When and how to say this? Routinely? In a friendly manner, cheerfully, encouragingly? How does one do that?
10. "Not a very good morning, is it? It's raining!"
    When and how to say this? Routinely? In a friendly manner, cheerfully, encouragingly? How does one do that?
11. "Yes, a lovely morning, isn't it?"
    When and how to say this? Routinely? In a friendly manner, cheerfully, encouragingly? How does one do that?
12. "Good morning. It's really hot, isn't it? Let's see, what shall we do today?"
    When and how to say this? Routinely? In a friendly manner, cheerfully, encouragingly? How does one do that?

These dozen variations on the theme (and there *are* many others) must be available for the teacher to use as need or opportunity present themselves. Nor should you treat the questions we have repeated after each of the above greetings as synonymous: When and how to say this? Routinely? In a friendly manner, cheerfully, encouragingly? How does one do that? . For these questions mean some three or four ways of **SAYING** each and that too a teacher must command. The **12** examples we have given mean at least **40** different expressions in **SPOKEN FORM**. It would be the same in any other language. How many of us command these **40** or so ways? And if we do not, how ever will our pupils acquire them for use with other people, and how will they acquire the spoken language?

Let us now consider another most common situation in our profession, asking a question. We normally treat the matter very simple-mindedly, as though there were only just the one or two ways of doing so. Let us take a

case in which we are checking whether pupils have done their homework or not. We would ask, "Have you done your homework?" and be done with it. But there are many perfectly accepted and common ways of asking the same question, each of which actually conveys a slightly different sense and also provides a change from boring repetition (you can replace <u>homework</u> with another item such as <u>reading</u> or <u>preparation</u>):
1. "Homework?"
2. "What about homework, all done?"
3. "Have you done your homework?"
4. "Done your homework?"
5. "Done your homework, have you?"
6. "Have you all done your homework?"
7. "You have all done your homework, have you?"
8. "You have all done your homework, haven't you?"
9. "Homework done?"
10. "Homework all done?"
11. "Homework ready?"
12. "Homework all ready?"
13. "Now, have you done all your homework?"
14. "Haven't you done your homework?"
15. "You haven't done your homework, have you?" ...

With these **15** questions and alternative ways of *saying* them, again we have some **40** or **45** more possibilities, each of which can be used either as just a variation or with a slightly different meaning to fit variations in situations. Each, of course, has stylistic and other limits on use, just as each contains grammatical and idiomatic variables. Importantly, one must remember that each of these patterns is **PRODUCTIVE**, which means that *other* basic questions useful in other situations can be varied in similar ways, both in structure and spoken form.

For one last common instance, take the situation in which we wish to turn to, shift attention from, or make a detour into a fresh topic. What does one say under these circumstances? It will depend, naturally, upon what has just been happening, how students have been reacting to it, how you have been reacting to it, whether it is

necessary to turn to the new topic, and so on. And to each of these possibilities also apply the crucial questions that applied to all alternative expressions we have looked thus far, **HOW** we are to utter them under the given circumstances, intention or objective:
1. "Shall we turn to ___ now?"
2. "Let's turn to ___ , shall we?"
3. "Do let's turn to ___ ."
4. "Now, let's turn to ___ , shall we?"
5. "May I turn to ___ now?"
6. "Look, we'd better turn to ___ now."
7. "Now, children / students, we are turning to ___ ."
8. "We are going to ___ now, so pay attention."
9. "Now we are going to ___ , so pay attention."
10. "Now, turn to ___ , please."
11. "Now, let's turn to ___ , please."
12. "Alright, we must turn to ___ now."
13. "Pay attention now, we are turning to ___."
14. "Look here, we are turning to ___ ."
15. "Enough of that. Now we are turning to ___ ." ...

Depending upon variables, these **15** (and there are many more) options may be uttered in at least three or four different ways. So we are again looking at **45** or more variations on the theme. These will not only relieve monotony, they will also provide children with models of the means of drawing attention and introducing shift in topic or focus.

Teachers and teacher trainers rarely acknowledge certain basic facts about speech. In any case, college teachers are not even required to undergo any teacher training and ignore these facts. First, without adequately clear Hearing, it is impossible to learn speech. Second, unless one develops hearing into the skill of Listening (i.e., hearing with purpose and with concentration), one cannot learn correct or effective speech. Third, Listening Skills are of two kinds:

(1) Listening to **Spoken** **Language**,
(2) Listening to **Written** **Language**.

By and large teachers ignore the potential of their own influence when they speak. They also tend to ignore the speech they hear, instead of learning from it, identifying better models or noticing mistakes when they hear them. Naturally, they are unaware of 'Listening to Writing'. This has caused enormous damage to English Language Teaching in India: here teachers keep speech and writing apart like divorced marriage partners.

However, especially for underprivileged learners from district towns and villages, the consequences of this oversight are drastic. Teachers regularly divorce speech from listening, and both from reading and writing. So pupils too implicitly believe in the distinction and keep these activities quite apart in their minds. They come to believe that speech and reading of printed texts have little to do with hearing and speaking. What is far worse, they come to believe that speech is *not* important. No one could be more mistaken.

From this mistaken presumption develops a harmful hierarchy in which they *order* skills the way their teachers do: Writing, Reading, Listening and Speaking, in that order, instead of being the other way round. The result may be experienced in the extraordinarily poor language control of millions of learners who leave our schools and junior colleges annually (whether graduating or failing). In fact, each set of skills ought to support **ALL** the others. When work related to writing is being done, teachers should remember that simultaneously *they* are speaking, and that pupils are listening. That is to say, teachers do not only lose such opportunities to train pupils. But they also create the impression that speech is separate from and far less important than reading and writing.

Since teachers are also products of the *same* system, this problem becomes a vicious circle. Our performance in class and outside provides uninspiring and ineffectual models for speaking and listening. Naturally, our pupils cannot speak at all or only speak extremely poorly. Listening to the text when reading silently, figuring it mentally in spoken terms, must become an essential part of our performance and teaching. Every activity of a teacher must show this awareness. For instance, listening to the full potential of speech in reading aloud is an essential part of a teacher's performance and his teaching.

To succeed in listening to one's speech, in making reading aloud an essential part of one's study and teaching practice, one must know what the pupils need to hear and how the pupils are to hear what they need. To appreciate this we need to recognize the following facts:
- Speech and Listening are two sides of the same coin;
- One must mind one's Listening Skills while Speaking;
- One must mind one's Oral Skills while Listening;
- One must mind one's Speech and Listening Skills while Reading Silently;
- One must mind one's Speech and Listening Skills when Reading Aloud;
- Indeed, one must mind Speech Skills even when just *thinking*.

If one does not mind speech skills even when thinking, **ALL** the **FOUR** skills are in jeopardy and a teacher's usefulness to learners reduces drastically. Moreover, to forget this crucial set of facts about language leads to loss of opportunities to
- teach new matter
- consolidate matter already taught
- refresh matter already taught, and
- test matter already taught.

But in our profession such opportunities are more precious than gold, and must not be wasted. Therefore, now let us look at how one must "see with the ears and hear with the eyes". For whenever a teacher opens his mouth, his pupils *are* listening to him; whenever he reads, they are listening to him; in both he is their sole model.

Whenever pupils speak he must listen; whenever they read, he must listen. Elsewhere, a teacher must listen to all the good English he can, from those who speak better and from trustworthy radio or television programmes. He must learn to listen to *mistakes* or poor quality language as well, so that he may learn from it and learn to correct it in his students' usage.

Clearly, we must appreciate that the skill of Listening to Written texts can only come after the skill of Listening to Speech. But what does listening mean, in the first place? Listening is *not* the same as hearing. Happening to pick up or perceive sounds is hearing. When one *directs* one's hearing ability to sounds *that* is Listening. Listening is essentially a *conscious* activity. That is why, wrongly, we generally speak of the Sense of Hearing but *not* of the Skill of Listening. Take a very common example from our daily lives—say we are waiting for someone. We **hear** everything that goes on around us, noises in the house, the water tap, the cooker hissing on the stove, the vendors out on the street, traffic noises, children quarrelling, and so on. But we are **listening** only to the sound of the door that will signal the arrival of the person for whom we are waiting. In theory, we hear everything. But in English we do *not*. For we did not learn this skill naturally; and we have not cared enough to develop the skill for our pupils. Listening involves everything from the smallest unit of speech to the largest unit of meaning in someone's voice—

1. Individual speech sounds (phonemes);
2. Combinations of sounds (morphemes and words);
3. Combinations of combinations of sounds (phrases, clauses, bits of them, hesitations, sentences, groups of sentences, types of sentences, and other units of speech or utterance);
4. Stresses *and* changes in stresses;
5. Rhythms *and* changes in rhythms;
6. The Music of speech (the tunes and changes in tunes we call intonation);
7. The complete structure of what we hear (whole 'speeches' and 'exchanges');
8. The meaning of each of these units of speech;
9. The 'grammar' of speech, which is always a little different from the grammar of writing, but for a teacher it must be a good indicator of the language his pupils have learned or failed to learn;
10. The meaning(s) between the lines (hidden meanings) of the speech;
11. The rates or tempos of speech and changes in them;
12. The volume of speech and changes in it;
13. The quality/qualities of individual voice(s) (or idiolect);

14. The identity/identities of speakers;
15. The identity of their dialect;
16. Even the 'colour' of voice that signals the attitude(s) of the speaker(s);
17. The total sense of what has been being said;
18. How it all fits into the situation;
19. Making decisions regarding what we are supposed to do about/how we are supposed to react to everything we heard....

Now you may see why there is a world of difference between Hearing and Listening and between Speaking Anyhow and Speaking Well. Even if our sense of hearing is sharp, our listening ability may not be. For that depends upon training, and interest; and for teachers, all this matters so as to help them identify opportunities to teach, consolidate, test and confirm patterns of speech. As we listen to speech and make sense of all these factors, there may be further complications in the situation. Perhaps more than one person is speaking. Perhaps there is a disturbance from other noises or speech. Perhaps we are preoccupied or busy. And yet, to be good listeners and speakers as *models* for pupils we must learn to listen to speech and make the most of what we hear.

A teacher who does not or cannot listen well will fail to hear what his pupils are saying and why they are saying it. So, he will be unable to teach speech constructively and relevantly. And thus he may deprive his pupils of **50 to 90** per cent of the meaning of all that is being said or heard. Thus one may deny pupils access to the most powerful aspect of language.

But it is never too late to learn how to listen and speak effectively. But you must now open your ears to the way the English language sounds. For nothing is too small or insignificant in this pursuit. Here are some useful hints—

Every morning, for a few minutes, seriously contemplate
- your role as 'sole model' of speech and listening skills for your pupils;

    start listening carefully and consciously to all the good speech you hear. (For instance, David

Attenborough on Discovery or National Geographic Television Channel; and people among your acquaintances who speak much better than you);
- start imitating first silently or just under your breath the good speech you hear;
- start listening carefully and critically to your own speech (in comparison to the available good models);
- correct your every mistake or unsatisfactory performance; systematically recollect all that you were taught or were supposed to learn in your Bachelor of Education course about English speech;
- refresh what you have forgotten or remember partially or incorrectly;
- acquire a copy of a genuinely useful and simple book on English speech (e.g., J. D. O'Connor's *Better English Pronunciation*, Cambridge University Press, a cheap edition with a CD). Read it thoroughly, and start *implementing* everything you learn from it, gradually advancing from small units of speech to larger units;
- acquire a copy of W. Stannard Allen's practice book *Living English Speech* (Orient Longman, India). Practise the patterns of stress, rhythm and intonation in it;
- acquire a copy of the *English Pronouncing Dictionary* (Cambridge, India). Start looking up and practising the patterns of stress in it.
- work with a genuinely interested and honest colleague to enable you to check each other's *actual* speech.

Of course, all this resembles learning yoga from books, never the most satisfactory or dependable procedure. But unfortunately we can do this mainly at second hand. So you *will* make mistakes. Modifications and improvements in your speech will seem to come very slowly at first. You will have doubts regarding the authenticity of your speech and hearing. So exercise caution at all times and be prepared to change again whenever you need to. You could, of course, with the greatest benefit imaginable, also listen to BBC Radio *because* it is a twenty-four hour service. Just tune in to it and leave it on at a low yet audible level of volume even as you go about your business. The sounds of the most varied programmes on it will keep washing over you, and you will learn what you do not even seem to hear.

You need to be aware that everything written also has a spoken shadow that is a key to its real and always complete meaning. If you neglect listening you risk failure in consolidating your speech skills. Colleagues who work in the same school can easily and profitably cooperate in this effort, as long as you do not mind being corrected by them, or correcting their speech. You could even organize a basic workshop especially in speech, with the help of college authorities or on your own. But without trying wholeheartedly, sensitively, with conviction and commitment, with sensitive eyes and ears, one will never achieve anything in this field. But if you do not, your pupils will pay a very heavy price, indeed.

You will be surprised at how few are the patterns that you must acquire to make your speech an effective model. The difficulty is in *hearing* right, *listening* accurately and *reproducing* sounds and patterns accurately and confidently. That is why we provide here a 'minimal' sketch of what is unavoidable, quite indispensable in terms of speech. It also constitutes the *first* crucial leg of a process that can only add power to your language.

The first concern is with individual sounds, simply because they are small enough to grasp, though not always easy to say or hear. English has **44** sounds that its **26** letters help to make. It is a language notorious for misfit between letters and sounds. (But *no* language can claim immunity from this problem, simply because **all** writing is a very poor record of speech.) Of these **24** are consonants and **20** are vowels. Some of them are easy enough to make, some are shared with your language, and some can be learned. A few are difficult because somehow they clash with patterns of your mother tongue. You will need to study a little to appreciate the details.

To be able to learn them really well, you either need an intensively available model or help from a description of how human speech is made and how English sounds are produced. But anyone who is free from speech or hearing defects can produce all of these sounds. Further, unless a teacher commands these sounds, pupils will never learn them. So learn them quickly and well. They are definitely among essential teaching items. Language is made up of *combinations* of individual sounds, chains of them that can be uttered together with more or less ease. To begin with they make up 'stems' or roots of words. Then next they make up words. Next they make up phrases that all go together. Next they make up larger units of language such as clauses, sentences, paragraphs or stanzas, and so on.

The crucial thing is to hear each sound—not simply think that one has heard it. If you know your mother tongue and your linguistic location, you can predict which sounds will be troublesome for you and which for your students. Study of such issues is called Contrastive Analysis. The point is to identify the sounds likely to prove difficult and teach them well before wrong sounds are learned. Once again, DOING matters, knowing does not. There was a senior teacher once who learned all the theory about English speech, for instance how the consonants /p/, /t/ and /k/ are aspirated (followed by an h-like puff of air) when the sound /s/ does not precede them. So she taught her class that in such places they must say [pʰ] and not /p/ in words like pot. Unfortunately, the moment she began to speak, she herself *said* [pɒt] and *not* {pʰɒt}! In teaching speech, dry theory is useless: knowing and teaching what must be said means nothing if you cannot *say* it! Among the **44** individual sounds or 'phonemes' of English, the most in need of teaching are the bilabial consonants /p/, /b/ and /w/ (as distinct from v); the friction (fricative) sounds of /s/, /z/; [tʃ] in church and [j] and [dz] in judge; the[ʃ] sound in shy, bush, etc.; the aspirates /p/ [pʰ]/, /t/ [tʰ] and /k/ [kʰ]; *not* aspirating any other sounds; the difference between 'long' and 'short' vowels (not confusing ship{ʃip} and sheep [ʃiːp]; there is also a difference in their qualities), and diphthongs.

But once one knows that, one does not know how to say every English word. One *must* know that the mouth must imitate a 'kiss' in saying the w in would and that only by checking with a dictionary or an excellent model would one know that soot is pronounced with a *short* vowel, *not* a long vowel. All such information a teacher can acquire from standard books of English pronunciation and not from books 'adjusted' to minimalist objectives. Learning how to *do* what one learns is the key to teaching. In speech a teacher must practise what he teaches!

Now let us consider very briefly and in a simplified form the mechanism by which human speech is produced. For you really do need to understand simple but crucial facts regarding the mechanism. [You must, of course, read a detailed description of speech production and classification of speech sounds.] They are not many:

The production mechanism: the human torso, with the rib cage, chest muscles, diaphragm and lungs, produces most speech sounds. [There are a few languages that use a few sounds produced in other ways, but not English.] These organs can squeeze and expand. When

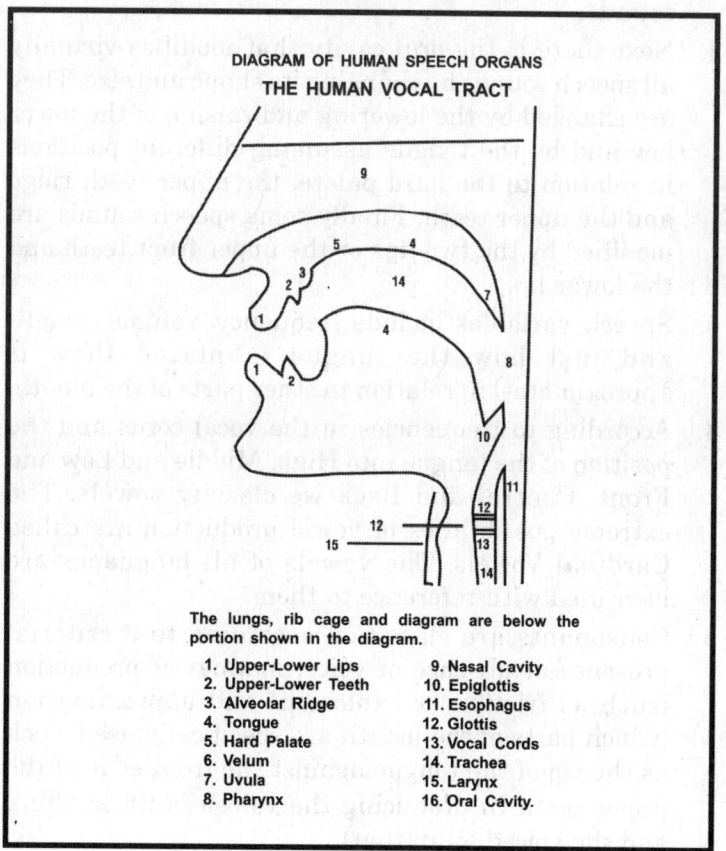

DIAGRAM OF HUMAN SPEECH ORGANS
THE HUMAN VOCAL TRACT

The lungs, rib cage and diagram are below the portion shown in the diagram.

1. Upper-Lower Lips
2. Upper-Lower Teeth
3. Alveolar Ridge
4. Tongue
5. Hard Palate
6. Velum
7. Uvula
8. Pharynx
9. Nasal Cavity
10. Epiglottis
11. Esophagus
12. Glottis
13. Vocal Cords
14. Trachea
15. Larynx
16. Oral Cavity.

they squeeze air out they produce the outward (pulmonic egressive) airstream by which we produce speech.

The articulatory mechanism: above the torso, in the throat and above are organs that modify the airstream. First in the throat are the double vocal cords, joined and attached at the front and open at the back where muscles can close or open the gap and hold the cords stiffly or loosely. This is the chief basic modification device. All vowels are produced here and further modified later. The essence of each vowel is a set of frequencies of audible airwaves. They are called 'voice'. Voice also forms part of some consonants, allowing us to distinguish between 'voiced' and 'unvoiced' consonants.

1. Above the vocal cords is the hanging and flexible back end of the hard upper palate that can shut off or open the nose passage. When it shuts the nose cavity, we produce oral sounds; when it opens we produce nasal sounds.

2. Next there is the oral cavity that modifies virtually all speech sounds by changing its shape and size. They are changed by the lowering and raising of the lower jaw and by the tongue assuming different positions in relation to the hard palate, the upper teeth ridge and the upper teeth. Finally some speech sounds are modified by the two lips or the upper front teeth and the lower lip.

3. Speech variables include frequency, volume, length and just how the tongue is placed (how it approximates) in relation to other parts of the mouth.

4. According to frequencies in the vocal cords and the position of the tongue into High, Middle and Low and Front, Central and Back we classify vowels. The extreme possibilities of vowel production are called Cardinal Vowels. The vowels of all languages are identified with reference to them.

5. Consonants are classified according to 3 criteria: presence or absence of voice, manner of production (such as friction or explosion) and approximation (which parts of the mouth are specifically used, such as the tip of the tongue against the front edge of the upper teeth in producing the voiceless {θ} in think and the voiced {ð} in that).

Once you begin to see *and* hear just *how* each sound is produced, you will have the opportunity to ensure that you produce the **44** vowel and consonant sounds of English.

Now let us consider very briefly and in a simplified form some basic rules of stress, rhythm and intonation *under normal circumstances*. The proviso (*under normal circumstances*) is absolutely crucial —because EVERY change in stress and intonation *automatically* changes *meaning*. So always remember, what you cannot do you cannot teach.

The Syllable

A syllable is the quantity of speech one can utter during one breath pulse. In perceptual terms, it is that combination of phonemes beyond which a native speaker does not break words even when speaking extremely slowly.

- All syllables require some energy to speak. However, not all syllables are spoken with the same expenditure of energy. Some are spoken with greater energy, or greater intensity, or greater loudness (or a combination of these factors) than others. The former type of syllable becomes **prominent**. Such prominence is *stress*.

Stress

- When strings of syllables are *spoken or uttered, some are strong or **stressed**, and some are weak or **unstressed*** (relatively less stressed—leading to perception of degrees of stress).

- Main or **Primary** stress is usually marked with a short vertical line just **above** and **before** the syllable in question. (Secondary stress is marked just **below** and **before** the syllable in question.)

- In English, stress is *crucial*, first because shapes of words (i.e. their auditory 'appearance', recognition and comprehension) depend upon uttering correct stresses.

- There are *six* categories of words (*substantive* words) which normally have a stressed syllable in them: *Nouns, Main Verbs* (and helping verbs in emphasis or negation), *Adjectives, Adverbs, Demonstratives* and *Prepositions in Phrasal Verbs*.

- Similarly, recognition and comprehension of whole sentences also depend upon production of *expected* patterns of stress.
- In such patterns, *unstressed* or weak syllables are grouped round (or 'governed' by) stressed syllables; they are *secondary* or *unimportant* in utterance. That is to say, the other side of giving the stressed syllables their appropriate prominence is the *weakening* or *squeezing* of weak syllables.
- Besides determining the rhythm of English speech, stresses also perform a most crucial function in intonation patterns—it is *within* stressed syllables that major and meaningful pitch changes occur.

Rhythm

- This leads us to the typical or characteristic *rhythm* of English. In English, in a given utterance unit (or a tone group), stressed syllables occur at *roughly equal intervals of time*. The prominence of stressed syllables, their occurrence at roughly equal intervals of time, and the necessary or consequent weakening of all other syllables together produce the rhythm of English.
- Therefore, each part of an utterance spoken as a tone group has its own peculiar rhythm, which is always governed by the necessity to utter the stresses at roughly equal intervals of time. The intervals themselves depend upon how many syllables are grouped around a stressed syllable.
- Its *rhythm* and *intonation* give English its *characteristic* spoken and auditory or heard quality. [Indeed, every human language has these properties, but each is unique in the *pattern* it employs.]

Intonation

- Intonation is that pattern of pitches in a speech act which provides a tone-group its meaning *over and above, or even well beyond*, mere words and grammar.
- No human speech occurs without intonation, in any language, at any time or in any circumstances; even a low monotonous delivery of an utterance conveys special meaning.
- Intonation has the power, in fact, of even negating the apparent meanings of words and grammar.

- It is the first speech phenomenon learnt in one's own language, and by and large the last one learnt (or not learnt or learnt very poorly) in another language, especially if it is learned late or from models who are, or have behaved (like teachers) as though they were, tone-deaf.
- Intonation being change(s) in pitch levels or 'slopes', the 'standard' or comparison against which 'change' is made or perceived becomes *crucial* in speech in any language.
- In English, for this purpose, it is important to learn the *monotone* or level tone in any pitch for comparison of pitch changes or modifications. The smallest changes can be made and detected against a level or *mono*tone.
- The fact that people usually speak within a narrow range of pitches—so relatively small differences in pitch have to be made and perceived to manage the language—is also important.
- Intonation being change(s) in pitch levels or up or down 'slopes' (or combinations of them), the locations where they occur under normal circumstances matter a great deal.
- These 'locations' of intonation change *are* the stressed syllables in a tone group. Thus stress becomes crucial for this reason.
- The way to understand and to treat a tone group is as follows (a tone group is a combination of words which makes a recognizable intonation tune with the pitch either rising or falling—there *are* combinations as well as levels of these, of *course*, but we shall leave them alone here):
  - Identify the *substantive* words in a tone group, part of a sentence or a sentence that will have its own tune. These words will provide the 'shape' of the group.
  - Identify and mark or check and mentally note the normal stresses in all such words.
  - Say all syllables *before* the *first* stressed syllable on a *low level* note or pitch.

This is known as the *Pre-Head* part of a tone group.
> Say the first stressed syllable, *and* all syllables that follow it before the next stressed syllable, on a higher level note or pitch.
> Say the next stressed syllable, and all syllables that follow it before the next stressed syllable, on a slightly lower level note or pitch,
> and so on until you have reached the *last* stressed syllable of the tone group or sentence. This pattern is known as the *Head* of a tone group (or, with two or more stresses a <u>stepping tune</u>).
> Say the *last stressed syllable* of the tone group or sentence with *rising OR falling* level of pitch according to the characteristic pattern for that sentence type or group. This is known as the TONIC crucial syllable of the tone group.
> Say all following syllables on a low, level pitch *if* the pitch of the last stressed syllable falls; say them on a rising pitch *if* the last stressed syllable rises in pitch. This part of a tone group following upon a tonic is known as the *tail* of the tone group.

• Here is an instance (a sentence with a *rising* tune) of the *complete* pattern identified above:

Is it good and proper that boys should be nice to insects?

With stresses identified, and its intonation pattern, represented graphically, the sentence will look like the diagram below. Remember that the graphic arrangement symbolises higher and lower frequency tones by vertical placement:

Is it **good** and **pro**per that **boys** should be **nice** to ↗**IN**sects?

---

good and
    pro-per that   s
                    boys should be   t
                                                        c
                                  nice to   e
                                                         s
Is it   **IN-**

➢ But **all** the possible patterns actually do occur. Here is a conversation to illustrate these patterns:

Just Tonic: (How do you want your tea?) ↘**PLAIN**.
Tonic + Tail: (Want some sugar in it?) ↘**CER**-tain-ly.
Head + Tonic: (And some biscuits, too?) **One** or ↘**TWO**.
Pre-Head + Tonic: (Is it good?) It is ↘**NICE**.
Pre-Head + Head + Tonic + Tail: (Like more?) It's e-↘**NOUGH**, really.

It's e-↘**NOUGH,** re-a-lly.

```
   N
     O
       U
         G
it's  e-    H  re-a-lly.
```

- Finally, specific types of sentences have characteristic intonation patterns under normal circumstances. That means that **ANY CHANGE** in the tonic tune **MUST** modify the meaning of the utterance from a minor to highly significant degree.
- Here are the main types of sentence and their characteristic intonation patterns **under normal circumstances**:

➢ Sentences that use a **FALLING TUNE** on the tonic—

(1) Statements, (2) Wh-Questions, (3) Exclamations, (4) Commands.

It is an e-**XEM**-pla-ry↘**A**-tti-tu-de.

In **WHAT MA**--nner will you pro-↘**CEED** now?

How↘**WON**-der-ful!

It **MUST END** im-↘**ME**-di-ate-ly.

Sentences that use a **RISING TUNE** on the tonic—

(1) Yes / No Questions; (2) Requests [usually with a fall followed by a rise in tune]

Are they **GO**-ing to ↗**VI**-sit us?

↘**Do** in-↗**DULGE** me in this, please.

Change the tonic tune and you change the meaning. For instance,

It is an e-**XEM**-pla-ry ↗**A**-tti-tu-de.

On a **rising** tune instead of the customary falling tune, the sentence signals a reaction to the 'attitude', either disbelief or uncertainty about whether it is really exemplary, or the feeling that there is something that counters it, etc.

➢ For another instance,

Are they **GO**-ing to↘ **VI**-sit us?

On a **falling** tune instead of the customary rising tune, this sentence will signal that you do not want them to visit, you are not looking forward to their visit, you are unhappy that they are going to visit, etc.

• In addition, if the rise or fall in tune are stretched, are **higher**, that conveys greater emphasis.
• When you wish to signal that you wish to continue, one example being the case of listing, the **rising** tune is used for all items of a list or where you wish to convey the sense of continuation *except* the final item of a list.

(1) At↗ FIRST, we knew↘ **NO**-thing.
(2)↗ONE,↗TWO,↗THREE,↗FOUR,↗FIVE,↘**SIX**.

Finally, move the tonic from the last stressed syllable to another syllable and you change the meaning by *emphasis* on the *new* tonic. This is called *contrastive stress* or *contrastive intonation*. In this manner, virtually any item in a sentence may be given contrastive stress to emphasize it or to correct the impression that something else was intended. For instance,

Did you say you can make anything?
No, I said I can *take* anything.

Now let us briefly consider what happens when we move into the realm of real speech, including speech as found in literature. Ultimately nothing is as important as this: for in language speech is power to communicate, and better speech is greater power. A dramatic poem begins with the following line: "Of course you can play with them." How is one to *say* the line? The normal way of saying such a sentence is

Of **COURSE** you can↘ **PLAY** with them.

But if the meaning is emphatic in response to the implicit question "Can we play with them?" then it must be said differently as follows:

Of ↘**COURSE** you can **PLAY** with them.

Consider another poem, Thomas Hardy's "Neutral Tones". In it everything is gray, because the mood of the hurt lover is gray. In the one-sided narrative, the speaker says at one point

> And some words played between us to and fro
> On which lost the more by our love.

I have had occasion to present this very sensitive poem to hundreds of college and university teachers of English. I ask them to "prepare" it for teaching. They do nothing that can be justly called preparation. But most importantly, they fail to see that they have a grave problem with these two lines **(7-8 of the poem)**. They ride over them oblivious that they cannot make head or tail of the meaning. When I draw attention to the lines, they are unable to see how the apparent problem with the *grammar* of the second line may be resolved. And indeed, that is hardly surprising. For here is an instance of the way grammar may be severely affected by how one renders written lines in speech. They invariably read line 8 as

<u>On which</u> + <u>lost the more by our love</u>.

We do frequently meet constructions like that. But in that case there is a serious lacuna in the line, arising from misprint or error on Hardy's part. But in truth neither is the case. The line needs to be read as

<u>On</u> +↘<u>which lost the more by our love</u>,

meaning, <u>on which of us two lost the more by our love, you or me</u>. As here, frequently sense depends entirely on speech.

Consider a modern and especially, even cynically dramatic poem of Philip Larkin, "I Remember, I Remember". Not only does it parody and extend the meaning of the earlier much anthologized poem of Thomas Hughes titled "Old Familiar Faces" the refrain of which is "I remember, I remember the house where I was born". Larkin's narrator happens to pass by the house and town in which he grew up. He remembers that he grew up there. He remembers Hughes' poem, too. Yet he recalls absolutely nothing of his childhood there, because, apparently, *nothing* happened to him there that was worth remembering! The narration and conversation he has with his travelling companion are ironic at the expense of all the things that are *supposed* to happen to a growing boy. Indeed, nothing did happen, as far as he is concerned. That is why the longish poem ends with a line to this effect: "Nothing, like something, happens somewhere". Now, on the background provided here and the sense of the narrative up to that point, how does one render the last line? A student in fact rendered it thus:

<u>Nothing like something</u> + <u>happens somewhere</u>.

If your command of English speech is even moderately good you will instantly divine that that is *not* how the line reads. You will divine that there *must* be two commas in it, bracketing a parenthesis. And you will know that the middle portion *must* be read like all other parentheses, on a slightly lower level of tones than the rest of the sentence, dividing the line into *three*, *not* two parts:

<u>Nothing</u> + <u>like something</u> + <u>happens somewhere</u>.

With the middle part said in a low tone *as a parenthesis* the grammar and sense are instantly illuminated: nothing (also) happens somewhere, just the way something happens somewhere. The line contains not merely cumulative irony but also a philosophical dimension. All that will be utterly lost to the teacher as a reader and therefore to him as a teacher; he will lose much pleasure and he will be powerless to convey that pleasure to his students, if he neither hears the enormous load of sense in the line nor manages to utter it.

You will see the point just as clearly if you consider a conversation in a novel. We read it and pass on, *assuming* we have understood *everything*. As though the arrangement of <u>word#word#word#</u> and so on alone makes all the sense. Consider the following small snippet from a narrative chosen at random from Nevil Shute's novel The Rainbow and the Rose (1958)

"Mind if I listen in?"

"Not at all," he said. "There'll be others coming to hear that."

Unless we are especially well attuned to the context of the conversation, understand every nuance of the relationship between the speakers, what has happened earlier and what happened a moment ago, unless we appreciate the interest of the speakers in the subject and their interrelationship and the direction of the dialogue, we simply cannot understand **50** to **75%** of its sense. How we *hear* the exchange determines the missing but crucial *non*-literal sense. Does the first speaker ask a merely routine question? Is he mildly polite or moderately interested? Or is he especially keen? These considerations will determine the exact tones of speech and the sense they are meant to convey. Similarly, is the second speaker nonchalant? Is he generous? Is he enthusiastic or warmly inviting? Each of these senses will force a certain spoken rendering of "Not at all", etc., without which we shall comprehend nothing beyond the mere words. We shall miss the 'flesh and blood' warmth or the pulse of the dialogue.

From these instances it is not far at all to the most dramatic language one can conceive of outside real life, say some speeches of King Lear: for instance, Gloucester's question, "Art thou not the king?" and Lear's utterly defeated and despondent response, "Ay, they told me I was ague-proof" (immune to fever)! Consider his dying words, "Pray you, undo this button". How shall one *say* them to bring the dying moment to life? Contrast his agonized yet suddenly once again brave and momentarily, pathetically powerful speech accusing some men of murdering Cordelia and threatening to avenge her death:

Howl, howl, howl! O you are men of stones.

How shall we render the agony of a once powerful, now geriatric yet royal passion? One cannot teach either ordinary language or such extraordinary language without secure command of speech. It is useless *lecturing* about Shakespeare's dramatic speeches. In life and in literature words never have only dictionary meanings. Dictionaries help us, but they hinder us by creating pernicious misconceptions: language equals words; that words have fixed meanings. Nothing can be farther from the truth! **Dictionary meanings are like grocery. We do *not* eat grocery.** We eat food. And food must be cooked and dressed for presentation. Cooking meaning is exactly what speech does, even when language appears before us in the written form. Not to know this, not to be able to read meaning beyond mere words and not to be able to render the language with the appropriate tone, lilt, emphasis, even colour of voice, utterly disqualifies a teacher of language.

From printed words with their meaning in chains to the necessity to make jokes, speak with irony, vary warmth according to listener and mood in literature and in life is surely the minimum necessary qualification of a language teacher. To voice the meaning implicit in chains of words, to do so in ordinary and in extraordinary circumstances, with flexibility and confidence—these are gifts that command of speech confers upon us. There seems no doubt at all about what a teacher of English must do: learn to speak as well as possible. His reward will be double: his students will outshine others and his life will be endowed with apprehension and communication of meaning that can only be described as the Power of Speech.

4 Computer Assisted Language Learning

*T. Ravichandran**

Introduction

The rapid development in the fields of information technology and communication network has significantly affected the social, the cultural, and the economical organizations of the country. The impact, however, has not been felt equally in our educational system. While society has spruced up to meet the challenges of virtual reality, and e-learning is fast becoming the new-mode of educating everywhere, somehow, the majority of the English language teachers in India are yet to come out of the British moulded dogmatic teacher-centered model of teaching. They are still reluctant to embrace the advancement made in computer technology and use it to the benefit of teaching language. But the need of the hour is to use the computer, multimedia and the internet to impart skills in language teaching, especially when young minds, caught by media–driven images and entrapped in the virtual net, have literally turned their backs to conventional classroom teaching. Superficial browsing on the internet for quick reading has replaced intensive, goal-oriented reading of books. In fact, the habit of reading books itself is diminishing. The same perhaps is true about the other skills of communication, such as listening, speaking and writing. Unless the teacher uses innovative, computer–aided teaching materials, he will not be able to attract and motivate young learners. Of

---

*T. Ravichandran is an Associate Professor of English in the Department of Humanities and Social Sciences at IIT Kanpur. He has published research articles on Communication Skills, CALL, Cybercriticism etc.

course, for the new generation that has literally become extensions of machines, anything electronic - mobile, laptop, blackberry, I-pod and I-phone - fascinates and quickly captures their attention. Hence, it would be more wise for language teachers to use Computer Assisted Language Learning (CALL) than to expect the present generation to fine tune to a *gurukul* kind of rigorous teacher-oriented, chalk-and-talk methodology.

Some Problems in Introducing CALL

Introducing CALL in a developing country like India poses some problems. Many of the teachers who teach English language are not technically trained to use software on a computer for teaching purposes. Although, on the one hand, there are some next generation internet–cum–computer techno-savvy teachers who are open to training, on the other hand, there are many others who are not positively inclined towards the use of computer assisted materials. Those who are skeptical about the use of CALL have probably limited computer skills and perhaps also suffer from technophobia. Yet, as a matter of fact, CALL does not need any specialized training.

The minimum skills by which one operates a television and a DVD player at home are enough to use CALL programs in an effective manner. This is where CALL distinguishes itself from LALL (Language Laboratory-Assisted Language Learning) where handling of the teacher console demands a certain amount of experience and a higher level of expertise. All that CALL needs is an open-mind and trust in one's own inbuilt teaching abilities. No doubt that the best teachers can be effective even without any technological aids. However, technological support from CALL, apart from adding to teaching efficacy, facilitates motivation for learning from the learner's perspective. Specially, in a language-learning environment, learners can *access* materials and experience interactions that would be otherwise difficult for a single teacher to deal with.

Nonetheless, there are external factors that deter even enthusiastic teachers from using computers to teach language skills. Whether one uses a language lab or computer for teaching language skills, one needs to spend uninterrupted hours and show intense dedication in mastering the technological tool, and to familiarise oneself with relevant software packages. In the syllabus-driven, course-coverage system that is widely prevalent in educational institutions, teachers do not have much time to spare to acquaint themselves with a new device and imbibe an innovative skill that can be used for imparting communication skills. Yet, one needs to realise here that the initial time invested in absorbing these technical skills pays rich dividends in the long-run, both to the benefit of the teachers and the taught.

Other interested teachers are disheartened by the lack of computer facilities in their schools and colleges. In certain cases, the computer facility is literally and geographically beyond the reach of a language teacher. Often computer centres are a part of the department of Computer Science or Mathematics and so the English language teacher has to adjust her schedule within the time and space generously offered by other department colleagues. Apart from this sense of flying in borrowed feathers, often the computer centre is at a distance from the office of the English teacher, hence, the teacher needs will and muscle power to walk to the computer centre to teach the language course there. Another problem faced by even motivated teachers is the fact that the teaching curriculum does not include CALL under the mainstream syllabus, which makes it difficult for both the teachers and the taught to pursue this as an extra activity. In other cases, there are administrators who underestimate the use of CALL and do not provide any support or encouragement to willing teachers. But all these problems are to be treated as teething problems and can be overcome once the concerned people realize, and convince themselves that the benefits offered by CALL outweigh its negligible limitations.

Freedom or Slavery?

There is also this unresolved debate whether the use of the computer in teaching amounts to slavery to machines of freedom in teaching and learning. Obviously, as a teacher who has been effectively using CALL, I subscribe to the view that it gives an unusual kind of freedom that is seldom experienced in the use of conventional teaching methods. Besides, CALL gives ample freedom to the teacher and the taught. While CALL enlarges the scope of language teaching, it facilitates individualized learning the students. The students can learn autonomously and can choose among the materials and set levels according to their pace of learning. In the mixed class containing extremely brilliant students and very dull students, the teacher often faces the dilemma of whether to raise to the level of the bright ones or to reach out to the dull ones. CALL can resolve this issue by showing sensitivity to the level of proficiency and by offering materials at various levels.

Paradigm Shift in Learning/Teaching

CALL offers a paradigm shift in the teaching approach as well as in the learning process. Literally, the monotonous and uninspiring blackboard is replaced by an interactive and stimulating whiteboard. The teaching obviously changes track from the conventional teacher-centered approach to the pragmatic learner-centered approach. CALL helps eliminate fear in the mind of a shy student and lets her work uninhibitedly. The role of the teacher here is to act as a facilitator. Interestingly enough, the special advantage of CALL software is that it enables learning even in the absence of the towering teacher figure by offering "a powerful self-access facility" (Philip 1986: 2). The syllabus in the teacher-centred mode is tightly structured, whereas, in CALL, both structured and unstructured interactive lessons give wide variety and freedom of choice to the learners. The objective here is not to "cover" the syllabus but to ensure that the learners enjoy the process of learning and "discover" something on their own.

Evolution of CALL

As observed by Warschauer (1996), the development of CALL can be traced in three phases, namely, Behavioristic, Communicative and Integrative (3). When CALL was first introduced sometimes in the 1960's, it served in the behaviorist mode by simulating language laboratory functions. The Computer in this phase replicated the role of the tutor rather than being a tool. Learners received instructional materials from the computer just as they would receive them from their teachers. Drills related to pronunciation, voice modulation, and exercises to enhance and imitate native speakers by way of active listening, were the sole features of CALL. Computers performed the role of a task-master by offering drills related to pronunciation and by giving repeated practice on stress and intonation. As rightly pointed by Warschuer (1996), "Programs of this phase entailed repetitive language drills and can be referred to as 'drill and practice' [or more pejoratively, as 'drill and kill'] (4).

Soon the growth of computer technology in the 1970's and 1980's and its incredible pervasiveness into all aspects of social life led to *Communicative* CALL. Rather than studying the structure of a language, and the function of grammar, the emphasis was on the use of language in communicative situations. The focus shifted from *linguistic competence* to *communicative competence* of the learner. In this phase, *skill* practice was given in a non-drill manner with a wide variety of choice, control and interaction. According to Underwood (1984), communicative CALL comprises the following premises. It

- focuses more on using forms rather than on the forms themselves,
- teaches grammar implicitly rather than explicitly;
- allows and encourages students to generate original utterances rather than just manipulate prefabricated language;
- does not judge and evaluate everything the students do nor rewards them with congratulatory messages, lights, or bells;
- avoids telling students they are wrong and is flexible to a variety of student responses;
- uses the target language exclusively and creates an environment in which using the target language feels natural, both on and off the screen; and
- will never try to do anything that a book can do just as well. (52)

With the fast pace of development of the internet and multimedia technology in the 1990's, CALL adopted an *Integrative* format in which computer technology is *synchronized* with the internet and multimedia to make the learning process *exploratory* and *experiential.* Thus, for instance, while listening to a piece of narration, the learners can also see graphics and watch animated clips. The skill can be incorporated with reading, speaking and writing as well. Lecture modules are re–framed as task–

programs meant for self-exploration and experimentation with language-learning in virtual worlds. Linked with the internet, the multi-mediated CALL programme caters to both synchronous and asynchronous communication between the teacher and the taught. For Warschauer, we are indeed in an *integrative* phase of CALL wherein we need to fully explore and exploit the immense possibilities of it.

CALL Programmes

CALL programmes are designed in an interesting and challenging manner. The basic sentence structure formation, vocabulary, and grammar skills are taught at various levels. Some of the popular programs are *Gapmaster, Matchmaster, Choicemaster, Storyboard, Wordstore*, and *Vocabulary Games*. *Gapmaster* uses filling-in-the-gap mode of learning, in *Matchmaster* appropriate words are matched, while in *Choicemaster*, the student has to choose the answer from multiple choices. Students enjoy using Storyboard as it uses the narrative from of telling a story to enhance language skills. *Wordstore* helps enriching one's vocabulary, while *Vocabulary Games* uses a game frame to boost word power. *Clozewrite* and *Closemaster* promote intense reading of texts in motivating the learner to win the games which replace the tedium of homework with interesting game-tasks. There are also some funny programs like *Facemaker* in which the learners assemble a face by using the English words associated with physiognomic descriptions. Overall, CALL programmes offer both guided and free-writing activities, and move from pre-determined to process syllabus.

LALL versus CALL

A Language Laboratory-Assisted Learning (LALL) programme is found to be quite effective in imparting listening and speaking skills. Nonetheless, computer laboratories have been replacing language laboratories by proving to be more effective and by using software that mix video clips as against the audio and the video tapes that are played only separately in the language lab. Unlike language lab cassettes, CALL CDs offer *interactive* programs. Language lab audio-cassettes as such do not provide any specific module to enhance writing skills. But CALL offers impressive programmes for developing writing skills and effectively integrates the four basic skills of listening, reading, writing and speaking. Today CALL is used to teach even soft skills related to aspects of non-verbal communication as learning to maintain the right facial expressions, postures and gestures and avoiding any distractive and negative body language cues.

Use of the Internet

Further, listening and/or speaking skills can be enhanced by connecting to web sites cum radio stations on the internet like the

British Broadcasting Corporation (http://www.bbc.co.uk/),

Voice of America (http://www.voanews.com/english/news/),

World Radio Network (http://www.wrn.org/audio.html),

Weekly Idioms (http://www.comenius.com/idiom/index/htm),and,

Learning Oral English Online (http://www.rongchang.com/book/).

Learning Oral English Online has Interesting situations created especially for those who are likely to land up in UK or USA for jobs or studies. The conversations cover useful topics such as 'Making Friends', 'At the Library', 'Shopping in America', 'Going to a Party', 'Ordering Lunch', 'Going to a Movie', and even, 'Dating'! Most of those sites also provide separate modules and materials to teachers for use in the language classroom.

The Future of CALL

Those who support and promote CALL visualize a utopian role for CALL in which it operates a constructionist and fully integrated tool. As described by Davies in the following imaginary scenario, CALL was visualised in the early 1990's by some business trainee managers as being taken to a very high level of sophistication for teaching language:

> A business trainee is sitting at a computer following a language course. Step-by-step, the computer presents the essential vocabulary and structures. These are accompanied, where appropriate, by still and animated graphic images, photographs and video

> recordings. As new words and phrases are introduced, authentic male and female voices pronounce them and the learner repeats them. The learner's voice is recorded by the computer and played back. Any errors in pronunciation are indicated graphically on screen. Offending syllables are highlighted and additional practice is offered on sounds which the learner finds difficult. At the end of each presentation sequence, the computer tests the learner's grasp of the new vocabulary and structures, marking and recording those words and phrases which have been imperfectly recalled and offering feedback on points of grammar that the learner appears to have misunderstood. The learner has access at all times to an online dictionary, a reference grammar and verb conjugation tables. At the end of the work session the learner's progress is recorded by the computer, which enables the thread to be picked up at the next session. In addition, the learner's progress records—along with those of all the other trainees following the same course—can be accessed at any time by the training manager.
> (Davies 1992: 113)

Although CALL has not reached this degree of ingenuity at the present moment, the time when it will reach it is not faraway!

Conclusion

There will obviously be some starting troubles when CALL is to be newly introduced in an educational institution. Also, gone are those days when it was thought that introducing CALL in ELT classrooms might pose difficulty for the students who lack the basic computer operational skills. Today, computers are being taught at first standard level! More than learning it from school, children learn these skills from the digital gadgets available around them by browsing TV channels, using iPods, playing DVDs or simply by tampering with the laptops at home. The apprehension that many teachers have in relation to the use of CALL is similar to the general fear that many people have with regard to the use of any machine in general that the machines will soon replace human beings and render them jobless. Nonetheless, instead of fearing this future, teachers should take it as a challenge and hone their teaching skills as well as reaffirm their own innate abilities. Teachers in the future, even if they are found spending less time in the classrooms, will still be needed for preparing CALL materials and resources. CALL should complement the actual teaching and accelerate the pace of instruction to make the learning process more effective and thoroughly enjoyable.

References

Davies, G. D. (1992) 'Computer assisted language learning.' In Embleton, D. & Hagen, S. (eds.) *Languages in International Business: A Practical Guide.* London: Hodder and Stoughton, 112-13.

Philip, M. (1986) 'CALL in its educational context.' In Leech, G. and Candlin, N. L. *Computers in English Language Teaching and Research.* London: Longman, 2-10.

Underwood, J. (1984) *Linguistics, Computers and the Language Teacher: A Communicative Approach.* Rowley, MA: Newbury House.

Warschauer, M. (1996) 'Computer-assisted language learning: an introduction.' In Fotos S. (ed). *Multimedia Language Teaching.* Tokyo: Logos International, 3 -10.

Contact Information for Procurement of CALL Software

Indian

- Young India Films, 1-F, Lakshmi Bhawan, 609, Mount Road, Chennai - 600 006 Mobile: 098410 - 22551; 098410 - 56109; Phone : 044 - 28 29 8693 / 4160
  Telefax: 044 - 2829 2065 / 5303; Email : contact@youngindiafilms.in
- The British Institute, UCO Bank Building, 3rd Floor, 359, D.N. Road, Flora Fountain, Mumbai- 400001. Phone : 2280755 / 22029541
- Linguaphone, Lotus Learning Private Ltd., F-13 FF, E.O.K. New Delhi 110065
  Emails: lotusbike2003@yahoo.co.in; Phone: 0120-2230935
- Focus Technologies, A-310, Sjovalik Enclave, Malviya Nagar, New Delhi-17
  Country wide Sales and Service Networks: Chennai- 9841022551; Bangalore - 9845168146; New Delhi - 9810240205; Madurai - 9841056109; Coimbatore - 9841056109; Trichy - 9841056109; Dehradun - 9897075761
  Website: http://www.focustechindia.com/

- Orell Technosystems (India) Pvt. Ltd., A-100, Amar Colony, Lajpat Nagar 4, New Delhi 11024, Phone: 011-32925999; Email: info@orell.in; Website: http://www.orell.com
- Sfeiiat Technologies India Pvt. Ltd., Sky Ways Building, Pottakuzhi Jn., Pattom P.O., Thiruvananthapuram- 695004, Kerala. Phone: 0471-4017501 to 10; Fax: 0471-406880; Email: marketing@sfeiiat.com
- Aditi Media Services, 474, 1st Floor 1st Cross, AGS Layout Subramanyapura, Bangalore-560061.

Foreign

- DynEd International, Inc., Tree Tops, Watts Green, Chearsley, Bucks. HP180DD United Kingdom, Tel: +44 1844 208 495 Fax: +44 870 134 8295; Website: http://www.dyned.com/
- Clarity English, General issues: Hong Kong office: PO box 163, Sai Kung, Hong Kong. Phone: +852 2791 1787; Fax: +852 2791 6484; Email: info@clarityenglish.com
  UK office: PO box 625, Godalming GU7 1ZR, UK, Phone: 0845 130 5627; Fax: 0845 130 5647; Email: melissa.pink@clarityenglish.com
  Sales issues: Contact: sales@clarityuenglish.com
  Website: http://www.clarityenglish.com/index.php
- GEOS Auckland Language Centre, 6th Floor, 21 Federal Street, Auckland, New Zealand, Phone: (64) (9) 303 1962; Fax: (64) (9) 307 9219; Email: info@akldlang.co.nz

Writing Skills

5 | Everything is an Argument: A Thematic Approach to Teaching the English Course

*Sharmita Lahiri**

Introduction

"Everything is an argument." We face arguments at all times or take our turn in making them as we talk or write. To be successful, we need to make effective arguments and understand well the arguments of others. "If arguments constitute such an important part of our daily lives, can you explain what an argument is and how do we argue in different ways?" with this question I began my first year English class at the Indian Institute of Technology, Gandhinagar. My intention was to challenge the perception of those budding engineers that the first year English class is a mandatory requirement which they need to simply complete, with little or no investment on their part. I put forward the question to make them realize that investment in it would help them within the academia and in their careers beyond it.

The course focused on critical thinking and effectively communicating the thoughts through the English language. The purpose was to enable 54 students - all very bright but for none of whom English was the first language - to immerse themselves in the language through reading and writing. From such an immersion they would begin to develop a fluency that would allow them to use the language more productively as a medium both to think and to communicate with others. A thematic approach was thus adopted; I designed the course as a

---

Sharmita Lahiri is an Assistant Professor (English) at IIT Gandhinagar. She obtained her Ph.D. from University of Houston, and had been a Postdoctoral Fellow at University of Houston Writing Center.

study of the purposes, strategies, and techniques of argument. Emphasis was laid on interactive, activity-based teaching, and continuous assessment. The objective of the course was to help students to,
1. become confident verbal and written users of the English language,
2. understand the value of specifying audience and purpose, and the selection of appropriate communication devices, such as voice, tone, level of formality, etc.,
3. understand writing as a process of thinking involving invention, organization, drafting, revision, and presentation,
4. recognize, understand, and apply the conventions of format, structure, and style appropriate to a variety of rhetorical situations and genres,
5. participate effectively in groups with emphasis on listening, reflecting, and responding,
6. understand and apply basic principles of critical thinking, problem solving, and technical accuracy in exposition and argument,
7. develop the ability to use writing and reading for inquiry; find, evaluate, and analyze different readings; integrate one's own ideas with the ideas of others.

These objectives were addressed through three main units, 1) criteria for effective writing, 2) arguments, and 3) implicit arguments. Public speaking and vocabulary development were focused upon, across all three units.

Unit 1: Criteria for Effective Writing

We discussed the characteristics that made the students like or dislike a piece of writing. Student observations were drawn from sources ranging from their own writing to the sports page and page three articles. From this discussion the following criteria of effective writing emerged:

- Effective writing involves thinking
- Awareness of audience, purpose, and genre
- Completeness
- Expertise
- Professionalism

- Clarity
- Correctness
- Consistency

Emphasis was laid on understanding that writing is a process comprising three distinct but essential steps, pre-writing (i.e. brainstorming/ free writing/ structuring/ researching/ doing background reading) writing, and revision. The difference between revision, editing, and proofreading were clarified as follows:

- Revising
    a. Occurs at the level of ideas
    b. Focuses on questions of purpose, audience, and voice
    c. May mean deleting entire sections and starting over
- Editing
    a. Occurs at the level of language
    b. Sharpens word choice and organization to make it as precise and effective as possible
- Proofreading
    a. Checks for accuracy and correctness
    b. Focuses on grammar, usage, and mechanics

Further, it was discussed that effective writing involves summarizing, analyzing, and synthesizing, and these three are again distinct steps. The following chart proved effective in explaining the differences:

Summarizing (The content is the same you put it in a different form. Turning Water into Ice)	
Analyzing (Taking things apart and looking into them through the microscope of the mind)	
Synthesizing (Combining your thoughts with what is already existing and creating something new. Water on iron creates rust, a new product)	

Unit 2: Arguments

In a short in-class writing exercise the students recalled an argument they had in the last three days. They identified audience, purpose, strategies adopted, and causes of their success or failure in making the argument. We went on to discuss different kinds of arguments (arguments to enquire, convince, persuade, and negotiate), and various appeals (ethos, logos, and pathos) used in arguments. The students were then assigned to write a letter to the Director of the Institute applying for paid on-campus work. Prior to submission, the writing samples were peer-reviewed. In-class discussion of student work focused on strategies of creating a successful argument to convince, and reiterated the criteria of effective writing and the importance of revision and proof-reading.

From our own arguments, we moved on to one of the most brilliant literary expositions, Brutus's and Antony's speeches in Act III Sc. II of William Shakespeare's *Julius Caesar*. The students were assigned to write a two page introduction to Shakespeare for an audience completely unaware of Shakespeare. The assignment focused on the importance of audience, and researching and presenting salient information in a clear and organized manner. In class, the students read out parts of the speeches and commented on their rhetorical qualities. Their responses to the well crafted arguments were enthusiastic and insightful. They discussed the rhetorical strategies that created contrast between the speakers and contributed to one outwitting the other. Parallels were often drawn with modern day political rhetoric. Interestingly, so absorbed had the students become in the speeches that Shakespearean diction did not pose problems of comprehension. Reading Shakespeare proved to be a good exercise in understanding the evolutionary nature of language and the power of rhetoric. The mid-term responses reflected adept summarizing, analyzing, and synthesizing of the speeches.

Unit 3: A Plethora of Implicit Arguments

In this unit, we read a variety of literary arguments in prose and poetry –"I have a Dream" by Martin Luther King Jr., "The Unknown Citizen" by W.H. Auden, "Blowing in the Wind" by Bob Dylan, "Psalm of Life" by Henry Longfellow, "Strange Meeting" by Wilfred Owen,

"The Language" by George Mikes, and the "Quit India Speech" by Mahatma Gandhi. The students teamed up in groups of four; depending on the length of the work, two or three groups took the responsibility of teaching the class a particular work, aided by me. It was imperative for every member of each group to contribute to the activity. The other groups rated the teaching on a scale of 1(lowest) to 5 (highest), and wrote a two to three sentence justification of the rating. This activity was an exercise in public speaking, team work, evaluating and analyzing different readings, discerning implicit arguments, and integrating one's own ideas with the ideas of others.

Across these three units, particular emphasis was laid on public speaking and vocabulary development through regular interactive sessions over the semester.

Public Speaking

The students teamed up in groups of two. In consultation with me, each group decided on a topic that interested them and presented their own argument on it for eight to ten minutes. The presentation had to be equally divided between both group members. The presentations were held on the last class day of each week. They began from the third week of the semester and concluded around the time we were in the middle of unit three. The diversity of topics was remarkable, and student enthusiasm for sharing with others what concerned them was apparent. The desire to excel before their peers resulted in substantial investment in the presentations. Prior to beginning the presentations, we discussed what constituted effective public speaking; at the beginning of each session, we reiterated the criteria and the students also discussed the strengths and weaknesses of the previous presentations. The presentations were evaluated on the basis of the following criteria: content, presentations skills, and overall effort. Since most of the students had already presented and received feedback on their presentations before they engaged in class teaching for unit three, a rise in confidence level and improvement in presentation skills, group dynamics, and understanding the audience's needs were obvious in the class teaching sessions.

Vocabulary Development

We started each class period with what we called "three words of the day." For each class one student volunteered to look up three words, previously unknown to him/her, explain their meanings and show their application in sentences. Throughout the semester, we thus compiled a vocabulary list. At the end of the semester a vocabulary quiz was conducted. Each student was given a list of words from the master list; he/she had to write the meanings and construct sentences with them. Using the examples given in class was not permitted. Since our vocabulary list was quite substantial, individual word lists were worked out for the students.

Mid-term In-class Writing and the Final In-class Writing

The day I began talking about writing as a process comprising different steps, a student had remarked that it was not possible to follow the steps while answering questions in an examination. His remark had remained in my mind, and accordingly I had designed the midterm and the final. In-class writing over two class periods constituted both the mid-term and the final examinations(See Appendix). I gave out the questions a week prior to both the mid-term and the final in-class writing sessions. The students could thus complete the pre-writing step before they wrote in class. They were allowed to use notes from the pre-writing exercise while writing in class. I took up their scripts at the end of the first session, and without looking at them at all returned them in the next class period so that the students could resume writing. The two day time period allowed sufficient scope for writing, revision, editing, and proofreading. The midterm required summarizing, analyzing, and synthesizing the speeches of Antony and Brutus. The final involved,

a. conducting an interview, and summarizing and analyzing this real life argument
b. summarizing, analyzing, and synthesizing the argument in one of the class readings.

Summary of Scheme of Assessment

Introducing William Shakespeare – 8%
Mid-term In-class Writing – 22%
Public Speaking – 15%
Class Teaching – 9% and Peer Review – 5%
Vocabulary Quiz – 5%

Final In-class Writing - 22%
Class Participation and Interaction -14%

Conclusion

The course approached English language teaching through composition and critical thinking, without resorting to the conventional method of teaching the English language through grammar and technique, which often descends to rote memorization. English was viewed as a skill that needs to be learnt through practice and error correction, rather than as a subject or knowledge system that needs to be learnt theoretically through rules and structures. The students responded positively to this teaching module. By the end of the semester they had become more confident users of the language. They had also realized that writing is a process that involves thinking, and the best means of gaining a level of fluency in English that will allow them to competently use the language as a medium both to think and to communicate with others is through reading and writing.

APPENDIX

Final In-Class Writing (Nov. 17 & 19, 2009)

You will write the answers to the questions in class on Nov. 17 & 19, 2009. All questions have equal importance.

You must pay attention to **clarity, organization and grammatical correctness**. Do not write bullet point answers. **I do not expect to see a repetition of the mistakes I have corrected in your previous writings.**

Question 1.
We have spent the whole semester looking at various kinds of arguments. Now it is your turn to analyze a real life argument. Here is what you have to do:
- IIT Gandhinagar is a developing institution. Interview one person who is associated with IIT Gandhinagar (he/she cannot be someone from our English class). Ask this person what is the one most important development that this person wishes to see in IITGN and why (i.e. how will this development help the institution and the students?)
- Now tell me

a) Who did you interview? You must mention the full name and the designation of the person. For example, if you interviewed a fellow student, write his/her name, year, branch and roll number. If you interviewed a professor, write his/her name and the department.
b) Briefly summarize what he/she said.
c) What kind of appeal did the person use?
d) Did you find the argument convincing? Why or why not?

Question 2.
a) Among all the readings that we did in class after *Julius Caesar*, which one did you like the best?
b) Summarize this reading. (If the piece is long, state the most important things)
c) Explain why you liked this reading the best.

 For this answer, I want the summary and the opinion written in your own words. So the less you will rely on the internet, the better you will score.

 You will be able to answer well if you chose the reading that you really liked; so the length of the reading should not be the governing factor in your choice.

6

How I Teach Paragraph and Essay Writing

Viney Kirpal

It has been observed that perhaps not more than ten per cent of students are good at writing. The figure could even be less. This small group is the one that has all the good ideas, grammatically correct sentences, smoothly flowing, well-connected paragraphs, and so on. Such students are the delight of any language teacher. But to have just ten per cent students who write well means that ninety per cent students in the class are weak. That, after studying the English language in general, and writing in particular for more than ten years, is a disturbing realization.

Writing is taught through school and college and yet most students shun it. They avoid writing because they do not understand how to get it right. But for the exceptional few who enjoy writing, the rest depends on bazaar notes to get through the compulsory English paper. The majority see writing as a 'subject' or a component of a subject called English, which somehow has to be cleared. It is neither taught nor learnt as a skill that is important to possess in professional life. The teacher's attitude also communicates itself to the student and plays a significant role in shaping the student's interest or lack of it. A good teacher can make a student feel confident about his or her writing skills while an incompetent teacher can fill her or his students with the dread of writing.

Basics of Good Writing

There is nothing difficult about writing if we can focus on teaching our students three basic aspects of good writing. These aspects are:
1. Teaching students the use of structure to write
2. Teaching them how to write a paragraph before teaching them essay writing
3. Guiding them how to write short, simple, grammatically correct sentences

Each point has been discussed at length below.

1. The first essential step of good writing is the use of **Structure** to write. If we want to teach our students essay-writing, it is not enough to tell them that their essays must have an introduction, a middle and an end, even though we have asked them to use some kind of a structure. Teachers who teach in this fashion only render essay-writing into a mysterious and unclear process. Unfortunately, a number of teachers teach this way. So do the majority of books on writing and they erode the confidence of the student permanently.

If we wish to instill self-belief in our students that they can write, then the primary point to impress on students is that they must *always use a structure to write*. By structure we mean a *framework* that will hold the different ideas cohesively together in an essay. This is easier said than done. So, it is necessary to demonstrate to them what structure in an essay means.

For example, if we want our students to write an essay on a city they love, how should we go about explaining the concept of structure? I could show my students the below-given diagram and ask them to complete it with their suggestions for content of the different paragraphs represented by three blank boxes in the right hand column. I can fill up the boxes one by one as the students make their suggestions.

Diagram 1.

Topic / Title	I Love Pune	
		Students' suggestions
Paragraph 1	I love Pune because	
Paragraph 2	I love Pune because	
Paragraph 3	I love Pune because	
Final Paragraph	Hence, I love Pune	

The teacher's role here is to go on repeating the statement 'I love Pune because—' and prompting her students to complete the statement with different reasons for the three boxes.

Topic / Title	I Love Pune	
		Students' suggestions
Paragraph 2	I love Pune because	of its climate
Paragraph 3	I love Pune because	of its cosmopolitan atmosphere
Paragraph 4	I love Pune because	of its easy pace of life
Final Paragraph	Hence, I love Pune	Sum total of paragraphs 1, 2, 3

As all the boxes get filled up, I tell my students that now they have constructed the structure or framework of their essay and all they have to do is to write out the individual paragraphs and sum up the three reasons in the final paragraph which will constitute their Conclusion as shown in the above diagram.

This diagram is very useful in explaining the concept of structure in an essay because the students can easily see that the essay is made up of a number of paragraphs with each paragraph taking up ONE particular aspect of the given topic. They can also see that the opening paragraph introduces the theme or thesis of the topic with a promise of providing reasons for it. The student further understands that the final paragraph is meant to sum up the various reasons stated in the preceding paragraphs. When taken stepwise through the diagram, the student develops a sense of connection, and structure.

One glance at the following diagram shows what the final essay will look like. Remember, I have not yet discussed the Introduction or the Conclusion because first we must teach our students how to write a paragraph. However, if the introduction and conclusion were to be added, the completed diagram of the essay would look a bit like the one below.

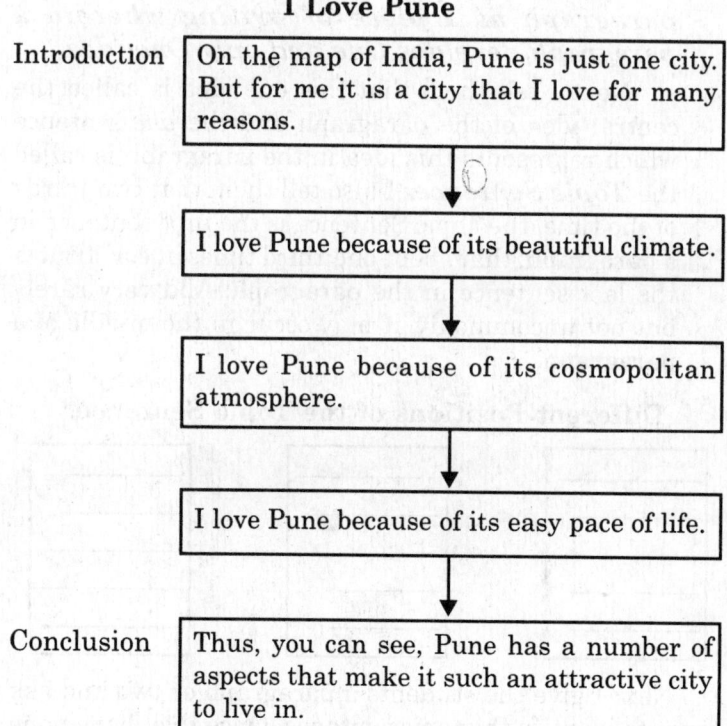

2. Having made sure that they have understood the concept of structure, in writing an essay ***the next step is to teach how to write the paragraph.*** This is because it would help the students know how to

expand each idea of the essay. I usually begin by asking my students the question, 'What is a paragraph?' Whenever I pose this question, all kinds of answers fly at me —some right, some wrong, some sheer guesses. But as a teacher I should be able to effectively summarize the inputs to help the students reach the conclusion that a paragraph is a collection of sentences which elaborates just ONE idea. Now, I must hasten to add that if a paragraph has two ideas, then it is not one paragraph but two paragraphs. This statement seems so obvious but it is not very simple for students to understand, at least in the initial stages and so it needs to be emphasised many times during their writing practice sessions. I repeat this point in different ways and through different exercises so that students can internalize the concept of the ***paragraph as a piece of writing wherein a paragraph develops One and only One idea.***

Next I tell them that this one idea is called the central idea of the paragraph and the *one* sentence which represents this idea in the paragraph is called the **Topic Sentence.** I also tell them that two-thirds of the time, the Topic Sentence is the first sentence in a paragraph, that about one-third times, it constitutes the last sentence in the paragraph. And very rarely but not uncommonly, it may occur in the middle of a paragraph.

Different Positions of the Topic Sentence.

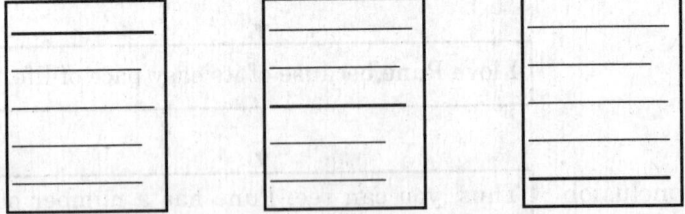

Next I give the students a paragraph or two and ask them to identify the topic sentence. Once they have done so, I ask them to analyse the role of the remaining sentences in each paragraph. This exercise helps them reason out for themselves that if all the other sentences in the paragraph elaborate and support the topic sentence, then that is the way to write a good paragraph.

This exercise is more effective if one can follow it up with a slide such as the one below to show them how a paragraph is structured since it confirms their findings. That helps them learn the point well. As you display the slide ask them to suggest how they would complete a given topic sentence such as "My Favourite Season" with supporting details. Insist that the details must be specific and not general in nature. You may need to explain the word *specific* with some examples.

Topic sentence

I am going to use the following specific details to develop this topic sentence. (Specifics usually include examples, analogies, data, evidence, etc. that effectively reinforce, develop and support the idea given in the topic sentence)[1].

Paragraph Writing

1. Examples: _____
2. Analogies: _____
3. Data: _____
4. Evidence: _____

The paragraph completed with the help of suggestions from the students may look like the one below, or you may have to write out one as an example.

My Favourite Season

Winter is my favourite season because it is so colourful. As autumn changes into the cold season of winter, people pull out bright-coloured woollen jackets and caps to keep themselves warm. When they walk or drive down the streets the lovely colours flash in the daylight and add joy to the environment. The most colourful flowers are seen to bloom in every park and garden. The purple pansies, the white, pink and violet sweet peas and the yellow dahlias spring up everywhere and turn the scene into a radiant painting. The richest coloured vegetables and fruits adorn the markets and malls. Bright red tomatoes and apples, oranges, carrots and peaches, white and red raddishes, ripe green and yellow pears temptingly invite shoppers to buy them and carry them home. Little wonder then that winter is my favourite season.

You can give the students an exercise such as asking them to identify the position of the topic sentence in this paragraph—'Is it the first sentence or the last?' 'Why do you think so?' Next ask the students to list the ways in which the sentences in the paragraph have supported the topic sentence. Thus we can give them repeated practice in understanding two main points that (i) a paragraph has its own structure and rules which have to be adhered to while writing it and (ii) that giving specific details (rather than general statements) helps develop the topic sentence.

You could also give the students two paragraphs, one in which the topic sentence is well-supported by the other sentences and the other in which it is not. The students can then be asked to distinguish the paragraph which is more effective from the one which is not and to justify their choice with reasons. Or you may ask the students to reason out whether or not a paragraph such as the one which follows is a well-written paragraph.

> Adventure sport is a fast-growing sport. Sports really contribute to good health. There is now a sports magazine in the market since last month. The relay race was a sport done thousands of years ago in older societies. People get injured in sports every year. Badminton players do not have a wide variety of rackets available to them. Playing sports can be expensive.

All these exercises can be given one after the other in different sessions to help students understand and learn the elements of good paragraph writing.

I would next ask the students to write a paragraph around a given topic. You can invite suggestions for topics from the students. This works well. Having gone through a proper training in paragraph writing you will be amazed at the ease and even speed with which students will now be able to write a paragraph since they understand how it is to be written. Before every writing session, make it a point to remind them that they should write just one topic sentence and ensure that all the other sentences in that paragraph support, illustrate and exemplify the topic sentence with specific, concrete details.

After they finish writing, you can ask them to underline their topic sentence and exchange their paragraphs with someone three desks away. That student will assess this student's paragraph. Ask them to evaluate the paragraphs for structure and adequate support to the topic sentence with specific details. The students can present their assessment of whether or not the paragraphs are well written and why. The exercise of evaluation is valuable in teaching students what to expect in a paragraph and how to judge its effectiveness[2]. They experientially learn about what constitutes a good paragraph and learn to avoid certain things which had turned another student's paragraph ineffective. Soon they begin to stick to the structure of the paragraph and write more and more effectively.

From Paragraph writing to writing Essays

You will have noted that all these exercises are designed to provide students with a framework to write the paragraph, since it is the most basic unit of continuous writing. Once the students have learnt to write a paragraph well, we can ask them to write essays. They can be taught to use a number of structures such as the Problem-Causes-Solution structure of the Analytical essay (For example, an essay on Delhi's Traffic). Another could be the Argumentative Essay which is constructed with the For-Against structure where a similar number of paragraphs are to be written in favour of, as against a subject. For example, 'Should Drinking be Prohibited for Undergraduates?' The For-Against arguments can comprise two to three paragraphs of each which now the student should be able to write easily.

This, however, will not make the complete essay because the student has yet to be taught how to write the Introduction and the Conclusion.

An Introductory paragraph is very easy to write if we ask our students to begin with a brief example or anecdote. For instance, the Introduction to the essay 'Should Drinking be Prohibited for Undergraduates?' could begin like this:

> My friend, Ashish, was only 16 years old when he began drinking. Until he joined College he had never thought of drinking. No one in his family had ever

taken a drink. But when he joined College he found many boys drinking secretly in their hostel rooms or at parties. One evening a senior ordered him to finish a glass of drink then and there, and he had to. Thereafter, he himself would willingly join parties where he could drink. Soon there was no stopping him. Today, at 18 is he a drunkard and though he wants to give up drinking, he can't. *I have been wondering since then why drinking should not be prohibited for undergraduates.* (Topic sentence)

There could be a number of arguments for and against this subject with lots of examples and anecdotes thrown in to develop the subject under discussion. **Arguments in favour:** The complete prohibition on drinking for undergraduates would be an important step in preventing young college students from drinking. This is so for three reasons. The student can present three paragraphs with examples in support of the argument. **Arguments against:** Prohibition has rarely achieved the purpose of stopping anyone, including students, from drinking. There are two reasons for this. The student can write two paragraphs in support of this line of thinking. After the student has written the arguments in favour of and against the topic, the student should be able to summarize the position he has defended so far. The illustrative conclusion could be: Thus, we can see that though both types of arguments are possible in favour of and against the topic, *the overwhelming opinion is that drinking should/should not be prohibited for undergraduates* (Topic of Essay).

From this discussion, it is obvious that writing the Introduction and the Conclusion can be treated as paragraph writing exercises with their own topic sentence and supporting sentences.

Assessment used to evaluate effective paragraphs, can be extended to judge whether the student has written the Introduction or the Conclusion well. The method I use is to focus only on one of the two components at a time and get the students to respond whether or not a student began with an example and introduced the given subject appropriately. Beginning with an example or anecdote of their own has the additional advantage of giving the students the faith they know what would comprise the first few sentences of their essay. Not knowing how to begin is usually a stumbling block with most students. But once they begin they can write the essay easily. Similarly, when the group is asked to evaluate the Conclusion they must opine whether or not the writer has successfully brought together all his arguments and summarised his point of view in a single sentence.

Using this approach, I have successfully taught paragraph and essay writing to some of the better and some of the weakest students of English. Once students understand that the process of writing is a scientific and simple one, they feel self-confident and are able to write independently.

3. The third aspect that teachers need to focus on after teaching the concept of structure and paragraph writing is enabling the students to write correctly. The most common block that students face is the fear of using incorrect vocabulary and grammar. They believe, and rightly so, that unless they know sufficient words they cannot write. However, the problem is not just of vocabulary. It is largely of insufficient control over the syntax of English. Students tend to use wrong grammar as well as to misplace words, even the words that they know. Once the feeling grows on them that they cannot write correctly in spite of having ideas, their diffidence mounts and they avoid writing.

After analysing a number of pieces written by students, I have come to the conclusion that most of them make errors in the syntactical construction of sentences because they are trying to write long sentences, usually literal translations of their thoughts in their mother tongue. All these end up as long, complex and compound sentences. Both complex and compound sentences are made up of multiple sentences which most of our students are unable to handle. They make mistakes when they try to express themselves through complex or compound sentences. In our classes, we teach our students to use complex and compound sentences because most good writing employs a variety of sentences. But my experience shows that the use of such constructions is best left to those who possess a high level of competence in English. For the average or weak students I have found it instructive to encourage them to express themselves in short and simple sentences.

Not to leave anything unexplained, I show them through a number of examples what a simple sentence (Noun + Verb) is. I also demonstrate to them how any idea which has been expressed in a complex or compound sentence can be expressed equally well by breaking the longer sentence into a number of short and simple sentences. I usually show them how easy it is to write more correctly when our sentences are short in nature because they have to use fewer words and their grammar is less complex to handle. The use of simple sentences to write paragraphs or essays works very well and is empowering for the students.

That is our aim, too. No amount of grammar teaching has helped the majority of our students to write correctly. If the use of short and simple sentences helps, so be it. Because simple sentences use minimal grammar, they enable a student to write with fair amount of correctness. For example, a student using both complex and compound structures wrote the following one sentence which took me a long while to decipher:

> If I am getting more things on same problem, say different way to prove, which one to be selected is not it missing something which was stated in other book and which one no.

The same student when asked to re-write this one sentence in a number of short, simple sentences was comparatively more clear and correct :

> The same problem can have many proofs. Different book give different proof. Which proof I should select.

Here the two obvious errors are the use of plurals in sentence 2 and the formation of a question out of a statement in sentence 3. Both can be taught. With practice the student starts writing correctly. The more important part is the self-confidence that their writing generates in students when they find themselves writing more correctly than ever before.

This method is to be used mainly with students whose competence in English is weak or on the borderline. For more competent students, teaching them how to play with words and sentence types is a rewarding exercise. One of my favourite exercises is to ask students to use a variety of adjectives when they write. For example, some students have the habit of overusing the word *nice*: nice car, *nice* house, *nice* job, *nice* salary, *nice* parties, *nice* bike. How about challenging them to substitute the word *nice* with different adjectives each time? You can turn it into a game where two competing groups take turns to give the appropriate adjectives. The idea is to create awareness of the need to make the effort to find suitable vocabulary in writing. This exercise can be conducted in a heterogeneous class. Interestingly, the other students also enjoy and learn from the 'game'. As their attitude to language and words changes, every body begins to enjoy looking for new words to use, especially, if the teacher makes it a point to praise their effort.

What I have demonstrated in this article is the need to systematically help students learn to use structure to develop their ideas, to provide concrete details, to use examples to give their own ideas to write grammatically correct sentences, to use a variety of words when writing. I have also emphasised the necessity of giving students ample practice.

Repeated practice makes the students more assured of the value of their own ideas and examples, and of expressing themselves through more grammatically correct sentences. What is interesting is that they stop depending on bazaar notes to write. Now you can be certain that they have been equipped to write good paragraphs and essays not only for their examinations but also at work when they become professionals. When that happens, our role as language teachers will have been truly served.

Notes and References

1. Framework adapted from Belts, I. D. and Howell, C.C. (1984). *Writing Plan*. Englewood Clifts. Prentice Hall.
2. High – level assessment of essays by students and teachers could include questions such as 'Has the student answered the question?' 'Is the answer insightful?' "Is the essay organized, coherent and readable?" For details, please visit http://www.informatics.indiana.eda/ under the rubric 'Criteria for grading an essay exam.'

Reading Skills

7 Teaching Prose

*Prabha Sampath**

Introduction

We speak and write prose all our lives; and we do not appreciate its versatility when it comes to teaching this much undervalued genre especially in a compulsory English class. Many people regard prose writing as not creative, because we use prose for ordinary speech and for the discussion of facts. This brings us to the crux of the problem: Is prose dull? Should prose mean boredom for the students and frustration for the teacher?

Prose is writing distinguished from poetry because it has closer resemblance to the patterns of everyday speech. The word <u>prosaic</u>, for instance, once meant 'containing prose or characteristic of prose'. Now it has come to mean something which is dull and lacking in imagination or spirit. That is the way we use it – unfortunately— though it need not be that way at all! Who would say such a thing of the *Essays of Elia* or indeed *The Diary of Anne Frank*? As teachers we would do well to remember: Everything in the universe of reading is in prose (except poetry) and we must be proud of teaching prose!

We teach the following fundamental skills when we teach a prose lesson.
- Reading
- Writing
- Listening
- Analysing
- Describing

***Prabha Sampath** is Reader in the Department of English of St. Mira's College for Girls, Pune. Educated at the Universities of Madras, Mysore, and at The Shakespeare Institute, Stratford-upon-Avon, U.K.,, she has taken her Ph.D. degree from Pune University.

We should ensure that they do not become empty skills! There are several ways of approaching the teaching of Prose.

Existing Approaches to Teaching Prose

1) Reading for Language and Literature: This approach assumes that students learn to read a language by *studying* its vocabulary, grammar, and sentence structure, and not by actually *reading* it. In this approach, lower level learners read only sentences and paragraphs generated by textbook writers and instructors. The reading of literary materials is limited to the works of great authors and reserved for upper level students who have developed the language skills needed to read them.

2) Reading Communicative Texts: Everyday materials such as train schedules, newspaper articles, and travel and tourism websites have become appropriate classroom materials, because reading them is one way in which communicative competence is developed.

3) Detailed and Non-detailed Study: This is perhaps the most favoured technique with school textbook writers and editors. It is also differentiated as the Intensive and Rapid reading sections in our textbooks.

The aims of Intensive Study are threefold.
- To develop vocabulary
- To gain competence in grammatical structures
- To understand language and through language ideas

Rapid reading has a different focus. It can have five aspects, namely:
- *Emphasis on the subject matter*
- *Reading for information*
- *Reinforcement of vocabulary*
- *Development of reading skills*
- *Reading for pleasure*

Most of us are probably practising these three approaches in class consciously or unconsciously. But the questions we must ask ourselves are: Do the various approaches serve their purpose? Do they cultivate a taste for reading? Are the texts prescribed suitable? Do they appeal to the students?

As teachers we face several problems. The first is an over-taxed curriculum. The second is *limited time, which means inability to do justice to the course. The third is the widely varying level of students' linguistic competence and the fourth is overcrowded classes. What we need to know is how to transcend or perhaps neutralize these problems so that prose teaching may be effective.*

The Fourth Approach to Teaching Prose

As against the three approaches mentioned above, there is one more approach. It is the 'Constructivist Approach' to teaching which emphasizes that we build on the students' experiences and their internal cognitive structures. It is essentially a learner-centric approach. The emphasis is on the learners – our students.

We have to use the constructivist approach to reading prose passages so that our students feel involved and motivated to read. However, before we begin, it is essential to ask ourselves a more fundamental question: Why do people read? Why do your students read? The reason we need to ask these questions is this: The purpose of reading is closely connected to the motivation for reading. It also affects the way a text is read.

As teachers we need to be aware of our students' learning needs, including their motivation for reading and the purpose that reading has in their lives. Talking to our students about the different purposes for which they read, talking to them about the different types of texts (stories, news articles, information texts, literature) which promote different purposes and forms of reading helps us to become more informed.

Why do our students read? Ask them that. It is very interesting to see what answers they come up with. Some of them will give you very idealistic answers – 'to improve my knowledge,' 'to improve my vocabulary' and so on. You have to sift the answers and arrive at the truth yourself but you will be surprised what it reveals. Some of them will simply tell you, 'We don't read.' So why do we need to ask all these questions? It is because I believe we must understand the student's motivation for reading. We need to connect to that purpose in order to reach anywhere and touch anything in their minds.

Often teachers try to push their own goals along, thus prompting the students' struggle for autonomy. For decades, educational institutions and teachers, parents and researchers have narrowed educational goals to learning and achievement. This has only frustrated students' social goals. It is time we focused on our students' goals.

I am sure we have students who are highly motivated in our class. They have already made up their minds about what they want to do. Some of them may be in English classes under sufferance. They do not want to be there and they think they know it all.

They think the teacher is not serving any useful purpose in their lives; they can manage very well with a guide or a class outside.

This is all built into their mindset. You can tell them — you can tell your most intelligent students that in your class, they will get practice for the CET CAT, SAT and GRE, because it all starts with reading! This will motivate them as they will see chances of their social and individual goals being realized. It will also help the teacher focus on the purpose of getting her students interested in reading.

As far as the teaching of reading is concerned, the purpose of reading is to connect the ideas on the page to what the students already know. If they do not know anything about a subject, then pouring words of the text on that topic into their mind is like pouring water into your hand. In other words, they will not retain anything of what they read.

To get students interested in reading, they must have opportunities to talk, read, listen and write in the class. For this, prose is the complete form. Students' comprehension is better when they are interested in the subject discussed. If they are not interested, what can you do about it?

Experts talk these days about a new strategy: The K-W- L+ Strategy

K stands for what you know,
W stands for what you want to know
L stands for what you have learnt.
+ stands for more!

Readers using the K-W-L+ strategy ask four basic questions while reading a given text.
(1) What do **I know** about this topic?
(2) What do I **want to learn** about this topic?
(3) What have I **learned** about this topic?
(4) What **more** do I **want to know** about this topic?

The K-W-L+ strategy has proven to be an effective reading strategy for both developmental and fluent readers, guiding them to think about what they already know (background), what they want to learn (purpose), what they have learned (discovery), and what they still want to know (planning) about a given topic. K-W-L+ helps both students and instructors engage constructively with texts and focus their learning efforts.

How K-W-L+ Strategy Works

Therefore, before your students begin reading a prose passage or article, it is crucial to introduce pre-reading activities. For example, if the passage is about drugs, you could begin by asking students a few questions such as 'What do you know about drugs?' 'Are there good drugs and bad drugs'? 'How do you distinguish between them?' These questions would guide the students to think about what they already know and rouse their curiosity about what the passage may have to tell them on the subject. Thus, we can introduce the topic in a painless, easy way, generate discussion when it has been assimilated and then start with the text. By now the students will know what to expect from the text and it will not be strange and unknown material to them any more.

Every reading comprehension passage has what are called ' Thin Questions' and 'Thick Questions'. Thin questions are those whose answers are stated in the passage. Thick questions are those which are meant to make students think. For example, asking students 'Do you agree with the writer's conclusion?' is a Thick question or asking students to suggest a suitable title for the passage is a Thick question. Both types of questions are important and help to engage the students at different levels of reading and comprehension.

Besides asking questions, the teacher can use a number of key instructional activities.

- Free writing to help students activate their background knowledge on a given topic and to inform instructors about it. (For example, asking students to write two sentences on the topic of the passage),
- Selected readings and class-level discussions to help students analyze separate topics and learn how to apply the K-W-L+ reading strategy and
- Summary writing to help students review what they have learned about K-W-L+, and to help instructors evaluate their students' progress.

The first activity, namely, free writing helps the teacher to gauge what students know about the topic. The second activity is about asking Questions on what they would like to know. A variant of this activity here could be Silent Reading followed by class discussion on key points learnt. The teacher can put down these points on the board.

Yet another activity could be asking students if there is anything more they would like to learn. The teacher plumbs this information by asking questions such as:
- Define the terms used in the article.
- What do you think the author means when he (she) writes '_____'?
- Can you identify examples of _____?
- What major points does the author make that you agree or disagree with and why?
- Speculate about what effect _____ might have on _____.
- How does the passage relate with your life and experience with respect to
  (a) the points the author makes about _____?
  (b) the ideas the author presents about _____?

By responding to questions that require different levels of thought (concrete, interpretive, abstract), students have the collective opportunity to analyse the topic, to share their impressions and ideas, and to ask questions of their own.

The Final Step is Summary Writing. It would involve all the above steps and activities and cover all the aspects of reading and learning a language. Writing is a form of thinking. Students are given the opportunity to think on paper, to put in their own words what they have learned from the page using K-W-L+ reading strategy.

At every step, we need to make the connection between reading and the students' lives, not merely their examinations. Experts have advised us to avoid monotonous practices and teaching methods in the class. They have urged us to use creative zeal to be flexible and to use our imagination. Imaginative teachers can make reading comprehension a useful and enjoyable piece of language learning.

How to Make it a Student-centric Class

One technique which I have found useful is simply to start off by telling the students to come and share whatever they have read, with the rest of the class. Tell them they can bring anything they like – it might be a newspaper cutting, it might be a story from a magazine, anything they found anywhere – just bring it to class and share it with the rest of the class. This would involve two aspects. One is the student will have to come up and read it out to the rest of the class and two, he or she will also have to tell the class why they found it interesting; and what made them pick up that particular story or news article and not something else. Their brief presentation can be followed by a class discussion. At least, when that is happening, everybody turns up, because they like to have their say. All I can say is we have to try every method possible to get them involved!

One of my most respected professors once said to me, "Stick to the syllabus alone, and you will be damned and your students will be damned." Harsh words, but it is the truth with English classes. If there is nothing rewarding in the syllabus, if the students feel that they really do not need a teacher to help them master the contents of the 'prescribed' text, then let us do something useful. Ask them what they would like to do in the English class. "Is there any way I can help you with improving your English? Are you interested in public speaking? Are you interested in creative writing? Are you interested in improving your vocabulary? Are you interested in free writing? Composition? Name it, we will do it." Let us shift our paradigm. If the students feel that there is nothing rewarding in the syllabus and they feel that they do not need the teacher to master the contents of the prescribed text, then let us do something more useful. Involve the students, give them what they want so that those competencies – reading, writing, analyzing, etc.—which we are supposed to be teaching them do not become hollow skills.

I must admit that this is easier said than done. After all, our students are going to appear for an examination at the end of the year, and we are accountable for their performance. But try and build these exercises into your teaching schedule. For example, organize a Group Discussion at the end of a lesson. Once in a while, you can choose the better students to come up and teach the lesson to their classmates. Let them have a go at it. Let their friends judge their abilities. Let them criticize each other constructively.

Let them bring jokes and read them aloud in the class. All this goes down as elocution. Let them try their hand at extempore speaking. It might be drama or playacting that interests them or let them try role play. Role play goes down very well with many students. Let them take on the roles in the lesson. Choose a character from the story or the passage and say to your students, "Pretend you are this person and defend your point of view." Anything you can do – and it varies from class to class and from teacher to teacher – anything you can do to get them motivated and involved can only be good for them.

Often, teachers (and parents) try to push their own goals along. For decades, schools, colleges teachers and researchers have had narrow educational goals to learning and achievement, which only frustrate students' social goals. Students must have opportunities to talk, read, listen and write in the class; they need to improve, polish and hone these skills. I firmly believe, prose is the complete form for this purpose. But it needs to be taught and learnt using interesting and innovative techniques. Students need to become the focus of the learning experience. It is time we moved towards the student-centric class. You will agree that we have to do our best to face up to the problem - - how to motivate, how to get uninterested students interested in what is going on in class. I feel there is no choice but for us to go a little out of the way on these things.

8 Reading Better and Faster[1]

Viney Kirpal

Fast reading is not about racing through a passage without comprehension or retention of ideas. Rather, it is a training in reading efficiently. Reading efficiently means reading with the least investment of time and with maximum comprehension. It is a strange fact that when we read faster we comprehend better than if we read slowly and with many fixations. Fixations are the number of divisions our eyes make in a line while reading.

Importance of Fast Reading

Because students of English cannot read fast, they find reading boring. And because they read little, their exposure to the use of written English remains pitifully restricted to the language they learn in the classroom. This situation can be remedied if students are trained how to read faster and with optimum comprehension. Such students would find reading a pleasure and gladly turn to a book or a newspaper and not postpone reading un-prescribed material. It is well-known that whenever students read voraciously, they increase their mastery over the language.

Presently, our language courses mainly consist of exercises in reading comprehension. The large number of available English Language Teaching textbooks bear testimony to this approach. Comprehension and communication are the primary functions of language use. Yet it is observed that most language learners in India are poor at reading comprehension. You will agree that this is so because, the student is rarely taught to read efficiently and or to comprehend quickly. Let me amplify this point.

In all English courses, the student has access to his or her textbook much in advance to their being tested for comprehension. So, nothing prevents him from reading it before class. In the classroom too, he is allowed to read and re-read the passage as frequently as he wants to in order to answer the comprehension questions. In other words, without even our realising it, the student is being almost trained not to read and comprehend correctly in the first reading.

What is the consequence? The student reads and re-reads and regresses, i.e., she keeps going back to read and re-read the same passage repeatedly without understanding it. This is obvious because had the student understood the passage in her first reading, why would she have re-read it? Re-reading prevents efficient reading and works to retard speed. This statement may surprise you but it is a fact that for most reading material one reading is enough to grasp the main ideas of the piece, irrespective of its length. If in addition to the main ideas, one wants to get the details, a second reading ought to suffice.

Often, you may have observed students reading a passage very slowly and vocalizing (i.e. reading every word aloud) and re-reading sentences they have already read earlier because they have not comprehended the passage. When tested for comprehension, they score very low. Why does it happen? Why do students score low on comprehension when they have read a passage repeatedly? This happens because in reading the passage very slowly and very carefully the students have concentrated so much on the individual words and created so many fixations that they have failed to get the overall meaning of the passage. It is like seeing a film slowly, frame by frame. Ask the people who read fast and they will testify that there is no need to read slowly. Reading slowly interferes with one's comprehension because it causes too many artificial breaks and fixations which only block the smooth intake of ideas. The question to consider here is, when so much is being published daily, is it worthwhile reading everything slowly when that material can be read quickly and with understanding? This is the first point for us teachers to work on.

Misconceptions about Reading

The second point for teachers to remember is to dispel some popular misconceptions about speed reading.

The first is the belief that we read with our eyes and understand with *our ears* and so we need to read every word and to read it aloud before we can comprehend a passage. But the fact is that we do not read with our eyes or ears as much as with our minds and brains. Reading with our eyes and ears is a physical act. It is only when our minds and brains are engaged that reading becomes a mental act. We all have experienced this some time or the other, when we read a page—every word of it – and yet were unable to recall a single idea because our mind had been wandering. On the other hand, we can remember every detail from a book that has absorbed us completely. This is so because in the first case, we were inattentive while in the second our interest had been so thoroughly captivated that we had given the material our utmost concentration. And so while we could not recall anything from the first reading, we could recall all the details from the second. That means that in order to train for fast reading, we need to discipline our mind and to rein it back to the reading material every time it leaps away from it in distraction.

The second misconception we have grows out of insufficient understanding about the range of our vision. Generally, we believe that we can see only those objects on which we directly focus our eyes. This is not true. To illustrate, suppose we focus our eyes on a calendar on the wall, do you think that we can see only the calendar on the wall or something else beside? Well, we can see not just the calendar but also the rest of the wall and the table on our left and the chair kept on our right. This is because our eyes have the capacity to give us a three–dimensional picture so that we can see more than we focus on. This phenomenon is called **peripheral vision** i.e. our eyes pick up objects right in front of our eyes as well as those on the periphery or the sides.

How does this information impact our teaching of reading? It helps teachers of English to recognise the fact that when we teach students to read fast, we must teach them to take into their vision not one word at a time but whole sets of words. To elaborate, when we read one word at a time, our eyes move and pause as shown in the example below:

This / is / because / our / eyes / give / us /a / three / dimensional / picture

Reading with a number of breaks, or fixations slows down speed.

However, when we read with minimal breaks, making use of our peripheral vision (as in the example below) our speed automatically goes up.

This is because our eyes give us a three dimensional picture

It helps us teach students to read words as units of meaning rather than as units of words so that the main ideas in the passage come to them in quick succession. When students read words as units of meaning, they begin to read paragraphs as units of ideas or concepts and grasp the meaning more completely than when they fragment a piece of writing into units of single words. As Buswell 1937: has stated in **How Adults Read**

> The most mature process of silent reading consists in the fusion of groups into units of meaning, which in turn flow into and become part of a large stream of thought constituting the total substance of the material being read. This process of mature silent reading is characterized psychologically by a complete absence of attention to words as such and by an absorption in the meaning unfolded.[2]

Bad Reading Habits Affect Speed

Besides training students in this technique of reading, teachers have also to help students break some common bad reading habits. These habits generally develop in students over the years and may need a while to break. Let me share these habits with you.

The first such habit is *vocalization* or the habit of reading aloud. Vocalization is a natural distractor for the mind, for when the student is looking at one set of words, his tongue is still articulating the previous set of words (our eyes always move faster than the tongue). Also vocalization forces the student to read at not more than

120 to 150 words per minute, the speed at which an average person speaks.

A variant of vocalization is *sub-vocalization*. Here the reader does not read aloud but makes lip-movements or engages in a kind of inner speech. Now, anything that resembles speech retards speed and sub-vocalization can be as much a hindrance to speed reading as vocalization. However, while it is neither possible nor absolutely essential to eliminate sub-vocalization entirely, it is possible to increase our reading speed by controlling sub-vocalization. So, this is a habit that we must discourage in our students if we want them to improve their reading speeds.

The second obstacle to speed is the habit of *regressing*. It occurs whenever we feel we have not comprehended what we have read and we re-read the text. It happens when we have not been attentive enough and have let our eyes wander down the page while our mind has been preoccupied with something else. Dissatisfied with our recollection of what we have read, we re–read it. But, remember regression is never necessary to reading; it is only a bad habit, it can and must be broken, if we wish to improve our students' reading speed.

How can we develop the habit of reading without regression? Well, first by insisting that students cannot regress or re-read even if they have missed an idea or a connecting thought from the passage. Secondly, by asking them to read on and to test their comprehension on the strength of what they have understood of the passage in the first reading itself. Compelled every time to read once, with concentration, they will, soon learn to read attentively and without regression.

Reading is a digestive process. If students fail to understand, assimilate or digest what they have read, i.e. they fail to relate it to what they already know, they will not be able to recall anything. As I am making a case for training language students in rapid reading it is necessary to state that one is not arguing for getting students to read at sensational speeds. Though claims have been made in some parts of the world of phenomenally high reading speeds such as 53,000 words per minute, and though theoretically every normal person has the potential of reading at 4 words in 1/20 second, that is, at 4,800 words per minute, it is not the purpose of this essay to suggest that we teach students to read at fantastic speeds. Rather, *it is one's purpose to bring about an attitudinal change in teachers and students towards reading* so that learners can be taught to read and comprehend more efficiently.

Different Reading Speeds

One's reading speed also depends on the degree of complexity of the material and the purpose for which we are reading it. Therefore, while training students to read better we must familiarize them with a number of reading speeds and strategies and help them to meet their varying reading requirements. For example, if their purpose is to read for entertainment then students should be taught to read at as high a speed as possible. If on the other hand, their purpose is to read for study, then they must be taught to scan as well as to read for analysis. To take an analogy, fast reading training is very much like learning to drive a car using different gears. If one wants to drive slowly one needs the first and second gears. If one wants to drive faster, one uses the third gear. And if one wants to speed up, one uses the fourth gear. Nobody ever drives in one gear. Similarly while reading one has to be trained in different speeds.

The difference in the speed of reading for entertainment and reading for scanning or analysis is very high. For example, while one can read upto 4,800 words per minute and more for the purpose of entertainment, one can scan a book of 300 pages in 15 minutes. When reading for analysis one may not be able to read more than 250 to 300 words per minute. This should illustrate the need to train students in reading with varying speeds depending on the purpose. Thus trained, they would be able to read with greater efficiency.

Methods of Training

With this I come to the last part where I wish to describe briefly how students of English can be actually taught to read rapidly and effectively. For a training in fast reading, we need to carry to class a set of unseen passages of varying lengths to the class. Use the first passage to record the initial reading speed and the comprehension level of the students. You can start their training with the very next passage. For this passage, set an incredibly short time for reading – such as asking students to read an unseen passage of 300 words in 30 seconds. Tell the students that it is extremely important that they read the passage within the allotted time even if they cannot recall a single answer to the questions to be answered. It is likely the students won't score more than 10/100 in comprehension. Some will even score a zero. Issue the same instructions for the next passage as well. It is almost certain that the fiasco of the previous exercise will be repeated. By now your students may begin to feel baffled and some may even want to know the purpose of such reading.

You can answer their doubts by telling them that in compelling them to run their eyes across the passage at great speeds you are trying to free them from the habit of reading with a number of fixations. Also assure them that with greater practice they will begin to read faster as well as better and be able to comprehend everything quickly.

Now take them on to the next lesson. Tell them that this time they must read within the prescribed time limit as well as answer questions on the passage correctly. For most passages, give multiple choice questions so that students can score them instantly. Sometimes, however, do have a variation like asking the students to read a passage and provide its central idea in one short sentence. An important rule to impress upon students is that they can read a passage just once and that they must not re-read it to answer the questions even if they are unable to recall a single answer accurately. Also ensure that all the students have access to the passage together, that they begin reading at the word 'GO' and after they finish reading they must record the time they have taken to read the passage.

As they continue to read a number of passages within specified time limits, they learn to answer most or all of the questions correctly. Within two weeks of such practice, you will observe that students have begun to show a remarkable improvement both in their reading speed and their comprehension levels. After this, there will be a period of latency when the students will not show any additional improvement in reading speed but rather will steady themselves at the enhanced speed and show an increase in their level of comprehension. Once the students have learnt to read comfortably at the new speed with a high level of comprehension, they will be ready to make another leap in their reading speed as they continue with the effort.

Along with a practical orientation in reading, the teacher should give short motivating talks on common reading habits and how to break them, on concentration and memory improvement techniques, peripheral vision and how to read with an increasing span, the method of picking up units of meaning etc. so that the student can utilize that information as he or she practises fast reading. A number of good books are available in the market. *Reading Faster and Better*[3] by Norman Lewis is an excellent guide for teachers. It is, however, advisable to select your own passages for the students in the context of their backgrounds and competence levels. Through sustained practice the students will be able to read more efficiently, i.e. in the least time and with maximum comprehension. Thus by training them in fast reading we can help students gain control over their reading material.

The next step in the training is to train students in different reading speeds for scanning, skimming and for analysis. The teacher should conclude the course with a formal test of the student's reading efficiency so that they know where they stand after a training in fast reading. It will be found that as students learn to read faster and better, they begin to read beyond the prescribed textbooks. By reading extensively they get exposed to a greater variety of structures and vocabulary in English. This will impact their use of the language in a positive manner. It will also help them in their professional lives where they have to read extensively in print or on the internet to remain updated.

It is important that students subsequently keep up the effort and practice of reading efficiently, otherwise they are likely to slide back into their former defective habits of reading. This fact needs to be emphasised throughout the course.

One final point. It is sometimes felt that unless a student is in command of a sufficient number of structures and vocabulary he or she cannot be trained in fast reading. I

A Common Misgiving

am sure you, too, have had this doubt. This is not true. For even as students acquire the basics of a language, they can be trained to form correct reading habits such as reading silently, reading with fewer fixations, reading with concentration so that they understand the main idea of the passage in one reading. In the more advanced stages of language learning, the student will have acquired a number of structures but he may still not feel confident with his vocabulary. In such a case, tell the student not to bother about a word he does not know but to read on and try to get its meaning from the context.

If, however, the passage contains many such unfamiliar words, then ask students to identify all these words first, familiarize themselves with their meaning and then read the passage once. It will be clear by now that your emphasis at all times must be on insisting that students read without regression, with fewer fixations and with concentration. As they learn to do this, their eyes will begin careening over the words while the mind will go on picking up the ideas swiftly. No student can fail to read efficiently after that. When I took a course of Fast Reading in 1979, my initial reading speed was 180 words per minute with a 40 % comprehension score. Over six weeks, my reading speed shot upto 784 words per minute and 90 to 100% comprehension. A 17 year old college student in my batch began with a reading speed of 150 words per minute and 40% comprehension. At the end of the course he was reading at 3000 words per minute with 100% comprehension. Such is the power of speed reading training.

An Experiment with Weak Students

Let me conclude by briefly telling you of my own experiment with teaching speed reading to a group of really weak students of English at IIT Bombay. This was the class consisting of those students who had been selected through the affirmative action system. Their English was truly weak. The year was 1980. I taught them the techniques of fast reading and gave them a few practice sessions, often taking with me copies of the Editorial article from *The Times of India* for the students to read. What happened was nothing short of a miracle. After just about 6 to 7 sessions, most of them had begun to read an unseen passage of 1200 words in two minutes and summarize the main idea correctly. The students experienced a sense of unparalleled exhilaration. Their improved mastery over reading also enhanced their grasp over English.

Conclusion

Fast reading and better comprehension is really about teaching students to read with a sense of urgency and deep concentration. As an example, let me give you a real life scene. Imagine you are sitting in your college library and reading a book because you need some references for your next day's class. It is closing time and you have only five minutes to read five pages. Would you be able to read them or not? Yes, you would! This is because the pressure on your mind to get the information is so high that your eyes move faster and faster and your concentration is at its peak. You will see nothing else but the content on those pages. If you test yourself soon after, you will realize that you remember everything that you had read with 100% accuracy. This is what is meant by reading fast and with comprehension. If you train your students in reading with a sense of urgency and concentration, they will neither regress nor vocalize. They will only read fast and understand well. This training can yield a very satisfying experience both for the teacher and her language students.

Notes and References

1. This is a modified version of a paper titled 'A training in fast reading for students of English language' (1980). *The Journal of English Studies.* 11/2: 737-43.
2. Buswell, G. (1937). *How Adults Read.* Chicago: University of Chicago Press.
3. Lewis, N.(1978). *How to Read Better and Faster.* 4th edn. Delhi: Binny Publishing House

9 Note Taking Skills
Niloufer Aga

Introduction

Learning is a very complicated process for those who have not been able to simplify it. Ironically, we have been able to make our lives easier with advances in science but not much has been done in the way we help our students learn in the classrooms. Most teachers are not equipped with tools or instruments which can effectively and effortlessly simplify the dynamics of both teaching and learning. Every professional has his own tool kit which he uses to work efficiently. Carpenters and chefs have particular tools for different operations. So also, we teachers need to develop our tool kit if we want our students to read, study and think independently. We can assist them in this by teaching them different visual tools to activate certain study habits. Helping students to sharpen their learning skills involves a systematic scientific process. This essay will elaborate in the coming pages, some of these processes for note making.

The Scenario Today

We find that there is a tremendous information overload today which the teacher has to transfer and the student has to receive and absorb. This leads teachers to dictate notes running into several pages and students to write them. Much time is lost in this process while students

---

***Niloufer Aga** is a Ph.D. in Sociology. She has been in the field of education for the last fifteen years. As an educator she has played a catalytic role in motivating and inspiring teachers through her teacher training programmes. She has been awarded the NCERT award for "Innovative Teaching Techniques".

get bored and de-motivated when they see pages and pages of words before them. Students then fall into the trap of mindless rote learning. Later, this becomes a habit which obstructs their progress as it does not prompt them to think. Therefore, English teachers would do a great service to students if they taught them how to make notes of their lectures in visual formats. Research shows that 80% of learners are visual. The brain is capable of absorbing 3,600 images every minute. Teachers must help students use their visual strengths. We have come a long way in using many new methodologies, besides the chalk and talk method. Teachers can avail themselves of visual tools and techniques such as Flow Charts, Web Charts, Mind Maps and Time Lines to provide notes to students as well as help students develop the skill of note taking. Through these methods, students would learn with greater understanding as well as be able to write their answers easily. I see this as the role of the English language teacher because her training will help students make notes in visual formats in all subjects. Examples from different subjects have been incorporated in this article to show how these formats can be used to teach and learn.

Visual Tools for Constructing Knowledge

There is a wide range of visual tools available for making notes effectively. These are as follows:
1. Brainstorming webs
2. Mind mapping
3. Time lines
4. Problem Solution format
5. Flow Map, Multi Flow Map, Tree Map

1. Brainstorming Webs

Whenever we begin a lesson, we can begin with a brainstorming web. Brainstorming webs get students to think about the various aspects of the topic on hand. While a student is thinking of ideas for working on a new seminar topic, he or she can brainstorm and capture those ideas in the web. Brainstorming webs also trigger off an open-ended network of ideas and associative thinking for the student. This method can be used by teachers to help students think on their own before they start teaching. How is this done? The teacher starts with a blank sheet of paper or with the blackboard. She begins at the centre of the page/ blackboard and records one by one all the ideas from the class and displays them in a visual format on the page or blackboard. The web branches out as the main idea expands with more and more ideas flowing in. For example, the brainstorming web below drawn by the teacher as the students contributed their ideas on creative writing.

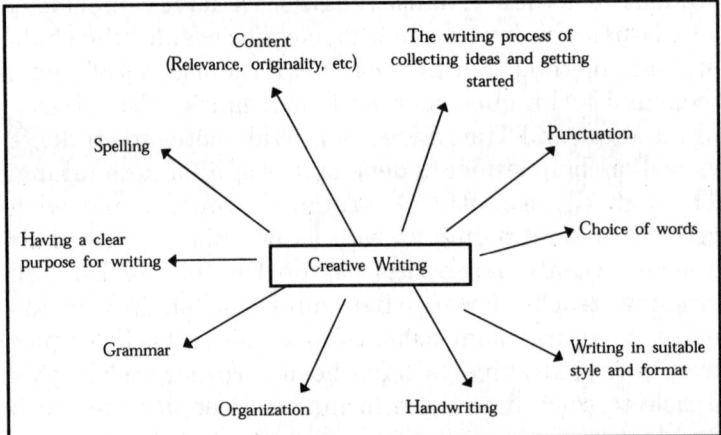

Or the web below designed by a teacher of Geography who got her students to brainstorm and think of the influence of the plains on economic life. She kept recording all the students' responses on the black board.

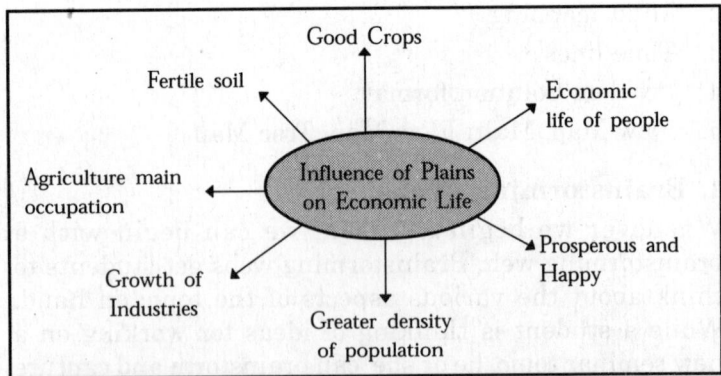

The Brainstorming Web can also be used to summarize. Once the teacher has finished a chapter or a unit, it helps to capture all the points/aspects covered during the teaching of that topic. For example, this is how a sub-topic from a chapter on "Dictators" could be captured in a Brainstorming web by their teacher.

This visual recording of points helps students view all the points together whenever required.

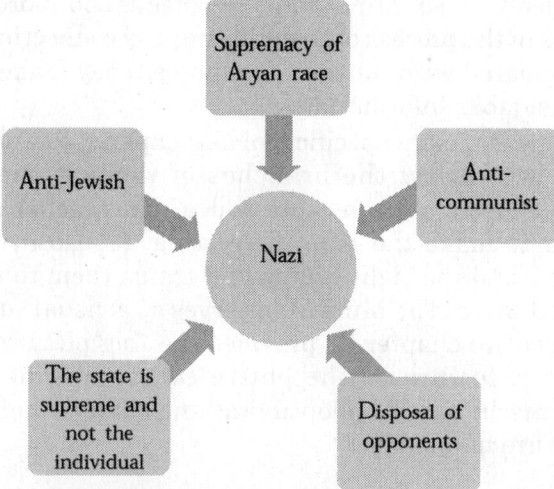

2. Mind Mapping

A variant of the Brainstorming Web, Mind Mapping was popularized by Tony Buzan (1994). Mind Maps eliminate the format of conventional note taking. They are organized by main ideas *and* sub-ideas. As such, a good Mind Map, shows the relative importance of individual points, and the way in which facts relate to one another.

Example

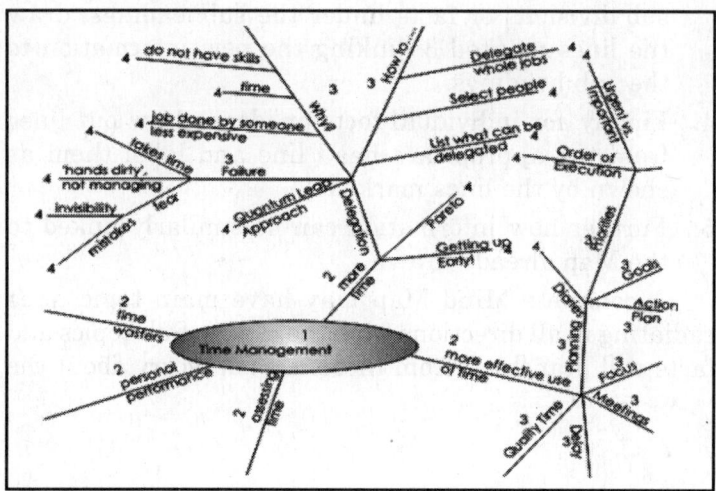

Mind Maps are more compact than conventional notes, often taking up just one side of the paper. This helps one to make associations easily. After having drawn the main Mind Map, if we wish to add some more information, we can easily do so. Mind Maps engage much more of our brains in the process of assimilating and connecting facts, as compared with conventional notes. They make it easy to remember information.

This is a more specific tool as compared to web maps. It shows clearly the branches of thought that have emerged from a given central idea. The teacher can use colour to make the map interesting. It also integrates the left and the right brains and trains them to work in collaboration. The Mind Map serves as a visual summary of an entire chapter. It provides the "big picture" of the chapter, lecture or the entire course and helps the students in quickly identifying and understanding the structure of a subject.

How to Make Notes in a Mind Map

To make a Mind Map, draw it in the following way:

1. Write the title of the subject in the centre of the page, and draw a circle around it. (See 1 in the above figure.)
2. For major sub-divisions or sub-headings of the topic (or important facts that relate to the subject) draw lines out from this circle. Label these lines with the sub-divisions or sub-headings as shown by the lines marked 2.
3. As you "burrow" into the subject and uncover further sub-divisions or facts under the subheadings, draw the lines marked 3, linking the new information to the sub-headings.
4. Finally, for individual facts or ideas, draw out lines from the appropriate head line and label them as shown by the lines marked 4.
5. Further new information can be similarly linked to the Map already drawn.

A complete Mind Map may have main topic lines radiating in all directions from the centre. Sub-topics and facts will branch off from these. Do not worry about the structure produced, as this will evolve as you develop your mind map. The idea of numbered branches in the figure has merely been used to explain how the Mind Map can be created and to show that only major headings radiate from the centre. What helps is the use of single strong words or simple phrases to convey information more potently as too many words could clutter the Mind Map. It also helps to print words on mind maps because it makes it easier to read. Using symbols, images and pictures helps students to remember information more effectively while using cross-linkages among the different lines of the Mind Map helps them to see how one part of the subject connects with another.

3. The Problem Solution Format.

The Problem Solution Format is a task-specific organizer. In this format, the problem is visually constructed so that students reach the solution in a structured manner. This means that a teacher may create a specific visual structure such as a blank map that students fill up as they proceed through a chapter. This format helps students to be systematic and focused as the task progresses. In this sense, it is different from the Brainstorming webs. Here there is no scope for bringing in various points. It is a bit like guided composition where the teacher provides a student with a systematic outline or diagrammatic outline which the student completes in an essay or paragraph form. The Problem Solution Format is a tool or organizer that helps the student to complete his task in a sequential manner. Providing the steps for solving a word problem or listing the steps for organizing content information in a research report. This format helps the teacher lead the student to the solution or desired write-up.

Given below is an example of the task-specific organizer to solve a maths problem by providing the different steps to be followed before arriving at a solution.

> **Q1.** Roshan is waiting at a stoplight. When it finally turns green, Roshan accelerates from rest at a rate of a 6.00 m/s² for a time of 4.10 seconds. Determine the displacement of Roshan's car during this period.
>
> Given: $v_i =$ _____, $a =$ _____, $t =$ _____.
>
> To find: $d = ?$
>
> Equation to be used $\quad d \quad \_\_ \quad \_\_ \quad \dfrac{1}{2} \quad \_\_ \quad \_\_$
>
> $d = \_ \text{m/s} \times \_ \text{s} + 1/2 \times \_ \text{m/s}2 \times \_ 2\text{s}$
>
> $d \quad \_\text{m/s} \quad \_\text{s} \quad \dfrac{1}{2} \quad \_\text{m/s}^2 \quad \_{}^2\text{s}$
>
> $d \quad \_\_\text{m} \quad \_\_\_\text{m}$
>
> $d \quad \_\_\_\text{m}$

Teachers report that one of the main outcomes of using this graphic organizer is that it provides a concrete system and model for proceeding through a problem that students would otherwise abandon because they have not developed their own organizational structures for persisting through problems. Once the student understands this technique, he can apply it whenever he needs to reach a sequentially logical solution. Since the visual structure reveals a comprehensive view of the process, it helps the student learn how to communicate his/her thinking with clarity and precision.

4. Time Lines

Time Lines help to visually capture the chronology of historic developments. Time Lines show events with dates to give a sense of progress in time of a process or event. They can be compared to milestones which we see on a journey. To summarize and show the major events, you might choose a Time Line. Given below is an example of how to teach the build-up to the American War of Independence using a Time Line.

Note Taking Skills 101

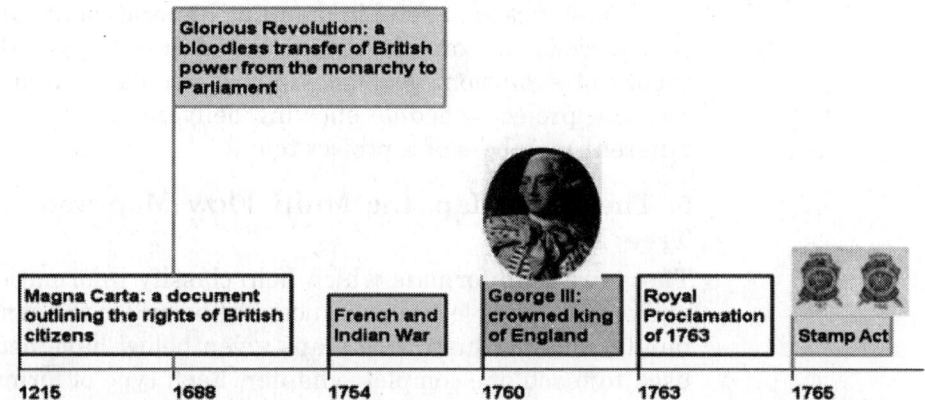

How are Time Lines created?

A horizontal line is drawn across the page, in a power point/OHP slide or on the blackboard. On one side of the line, you mention the dates while on the other side you record the corresponding events. Pictures of the events can be added to make the Time Lines colourful and interesting for the student. In the above example the first date and event plotted on the Time Line is the beginning of the period in History that you want to depict. The last date and event will depict the end point of the period being discussed in the chapter or topic.

Time Lines have several uses. They help to arrange past events chronologically. For example, innovations in science between 1800 and 2000, or to represent a person's life history. For example, the life of Alexander the Great:

Build-up to the American War of Independence

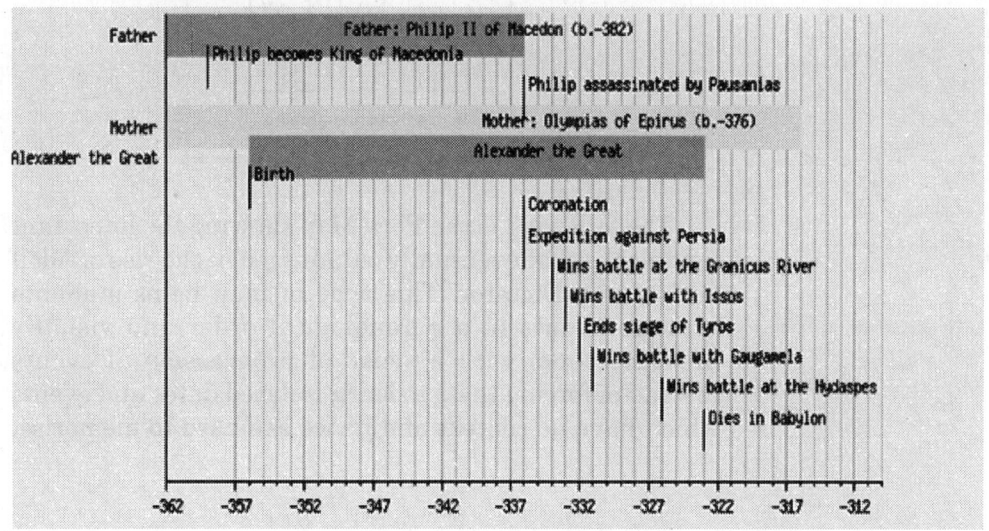

Time Lines are useful in mapping historic events and time periods for example, the history of the universe, the theory of evolution, geologic time. A popular use is to create a project schedule showing deliverable dates for different members of a project team.

5. The Flow Map, the Multi Flow Map and the Tree Map

These are map formats which help classify information and enable quick learning. Since they belong to the same family, all the illustrative maps given below have been used to teach one complete chapter. Each type of format or map has been discussed below and then exemplified by taking the content from the chapter 'The Rise of Dictatorships' taken from the First Year B.A., Pune University, History text book 0(2.1-2.18).

i. **Flow Maps** are used to sequence a process from start to finish. They identify the relationships between stages and sub-stages of procedure (or order or number of operations or steps, etc.). For example, how a caterpillar becomes a butterfly, how global warming is going to affect us, how the economic melt-down has been affecting the world. Given below is the stick model of a Flow Map demonstrating the sequence and flow of events.

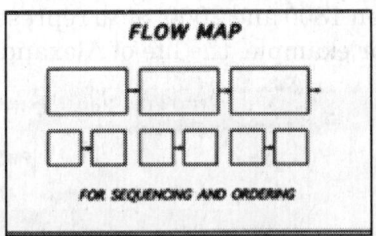

The following is the Flow Map showing the important landmarks that eventually culminated in the rise of Adolf Hitler as a Dictator. This type of map helps students arrange events in a chronological order and visually provides them with a sense of progression of events instead of forcing them to learn isolated dates and events which have no context and hence are hard to memorise.

Note Taking Skills

The Rise of Adolf Hitler as a Dictator

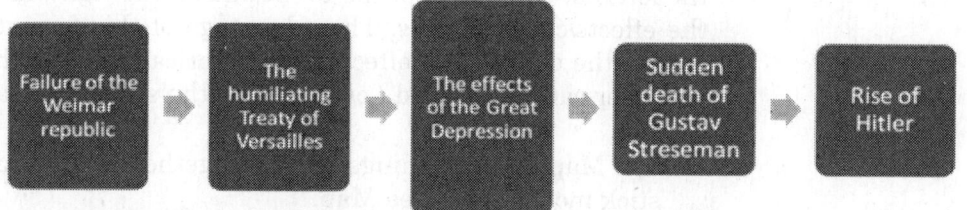

How a Flow Map is Constructed

In the outer rectangle, write the name of the event or sequence. Subsequent rectangles list the steps or events that have occurred from the beginning to the end (See the above figure). Smaller rectangles may be drawn below to list sub-stages.

Using a Flow Map is good practice for students to think logically and as a whole about the topic. It also helps in recalling the order of events, as in a story. This is especially useful for teachers while teaching literature or comprehension passages to students. Teachers can use the Flow Map effectively to teach the history of a topic in any discipline. It can be used to give directions to someone and see if they can follow them. For practice, teachers can have students make a Flow Map explaining how to repair a computer, access books in the library or fill up admission forms.

ii. Multi-Flow Maps are used to represent causes and effects of events. It is a process of sequencing that looks at what caused an event and the results/effects of the event. It helps pupils analyse a situation by looking at the cause and effect – the 'why' and 'consequences' good or bad. For example, analysing friends or peers or fictional characters.

Given below is the stick model of a Multi Flow map.

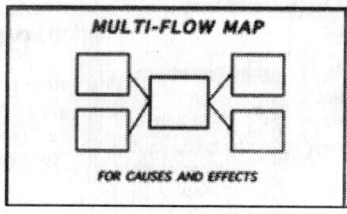

To construct a Multi-Flow Map list the event that has occurred in the centre of the rectangle. In the boxes on the left, list the causes of the event and on the right, list the effects/consequences. The advantage of this format is that the causes and effects of a historical event such as Hitler can be grasped / captured by the student at a glance.

iii. Tree Maps classify things or ideas together. Below is a stick model for a Tree Map.

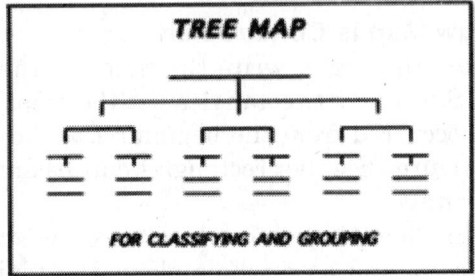

How is a Tree Map Constructed? On the top line, write the category name. Below that begin writing sub-categories. Below each sub-category write specific members of the group. The Tree Map below visually gives the students all the major aspects of the three Dictators of Europe during World War I, namely, General Franco, Mussolini and Hitler. This makes it very easy for them to remember and recall the details.

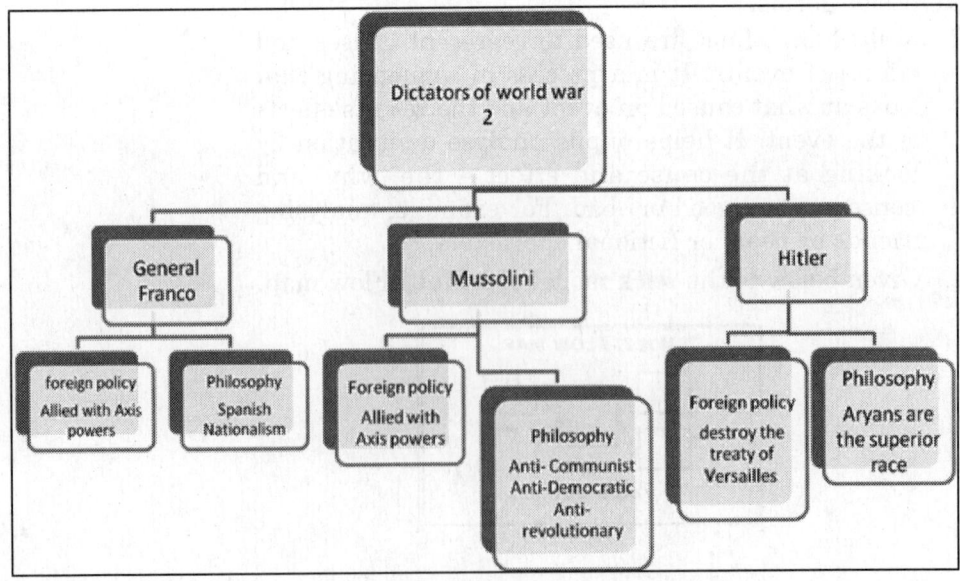

The Tree Map can be used to teach study topics in English (for example, spellings and words), Geography, Science, History, Sociology by grouping similar categories. For class exercise, you could ask the students to make a shopping list for the supermarket and organise it by type of food (i.e. produce, dairy, canned goods, treats, etc.).

Conclusion

All the tools described so far can be used one by one. These can also be brought together on one large sheet so that the student can get the big picture of a topic, chapter or subject at a glance. English teachers train students how to make and use tools such as the Brainstorming Web Chart, the Mind Map, Time Lines, the Tree Map, the Flow Map, the Multi Flow Map and the Problem Solving Format by example and guided practice. All these tools can be applied across disciplines. These maps can also be used as evaluation tools by the teacher, as well as to train a student to thoughtfully organize the material to be studied.

References

Buzan, T(1994) *Use Both Sides of Your Brain*. London: Dutton.
Costa, A.(1991) *Patterns of Thinking*. New York: Association for Supervision and Curriculum Development.
Hyerle, D(1996) *Visual Tools for Constructing Knowledge*. Alexandra: Association for Supervision and Curriculum Development.
Rajan, S and Dasture, P (2008.) *The World After World War - 1:1918 -1992*. Chapter 2 'Rise of Dictatorships' pp 2.1 to 2.18. First Year B.A. History Textbook prescribed under the new Syllabus of Pune University, since 2008. Pune: Nirali Prakashan. 2008.
Websites
www.tutorvista.com
ww.lifestreasmcenter.net/.../thinking maps.htm
http:/www.bucks.edu/~specpop/visual-org.htm

Grammar and Word Power Development

10 Teaching of Grammar

Shridhar B. Gokhale

Introduction

Grammar is the underlying system of a language and is often viewed as the central mechanism of a language. All the languages and all the varieties of a language have their own grammars. Teaching of a language is often equated with the teaching of grammar and it is sometimes thought that a conscious knowledge of grammar is essential for the use of a language.

Knowing a Language and Knowing about a Language

A distinction must be made between knowing a language and knowing about a language. Everyone knows his first language very well, but he may not necessarily know much about it. Knowing a language is being able to use the language successfully in different situations and it involves the four basic language skills of listening, speaking, reading and writing. Knowing about a language means having a lot of information about a language and being able to describe and explain the facts of a language. Obviously, what is useful for most people is knowing a language and only a few people like linguists and teachers need to know about a language, often in addition to knowing it.

There are parallel distinctions between learning a language and learning about a language, studying a language and studying about a language, and teaching a language and teaching about a language. In all these cases the former involves an unconscious and implicit knowledge of grammar, whereas the latter involves its conscious and explicit knowledge.

Why is a Student Taught English for a Long Time in India?

An average Indian student learns English for about 11 to15 years – at least six years at school, two years in the Junior College and three years in the Senior College – and still at the end of all this, his competence in English is extremely poor because he cannot introduce himself effectively to an audience nor can he write a faultless application for a job. A major factor responsible for this is that most of the teaching of English in India is teaching about English and not really teaching of English. The teacher usually imparts a lot of information about the language, but this does not lead to the mastery of basic language skills on the part of the learners.

Teaching of Grammar and Teaching about English

Explicit teaching of grammar is synonymous with teaching about English, because it involves giving students the rules of grammar and giving them practice in applying those rules. There is a misunderstanding about remedial teaching in India. Both teachers and students wrongly believe that remedial teaching entails teaching and learning of grammar once again. It is not being suggested here that teaching about a language is a totally irrelevant and insignificant activity. It has its own limited uses, particularly in the second/foreign language situation. However, it must be ensured that in all situations, teaching about a language leads to teaching of the language. In other words, teaching grammar is only a means to an end. It must not be done for its own sake. It can justifiably be done only as one of the ways of making students learn the language efficiently. It is certainly possible to teach a language without explicitly teaching grammar. This can be done by providing copious exposure to the use of language, opportunities to use the language in real-life situations, freedom for students to make errors and encouragement to correct themselves. This involves teaching grammar implicitly and unconsciously. It makes the experience of learning grammar an enjoyable one.

Form and Function in the Teaching of Grammar

Every grammatical construction has two important aspects — form and function. Form refers to the structure of a sentence and the manner of its formation. Function, on the other hand, refers to how the sentence is used in day-to-day life and how we can perform various actions by using the sentence. For example, 'Could you pass the salt, please?'

From the point of view of form, this sentence is a yes-no question, as it begins with an operator, it involves S-V inversion and it would normally be said with a rising intonation. All these features relate to the construction of the sentence and hence are formal features of the sentence. However, from the point of view of function, the sentence is a polite request made to the listener. Functionally, it is not a yes-no question and cannot be answered just in terms of 'yes' or 'no'. The most appropriate response to this is the action of passing the salt, optionally accompanied by an utterance like 'Certainly'.

It has been observed that the teacher of English in India gives greater importance to formal grammar and almost ignores the functional aspect of grammar. He spends a lot of time and energy on the explanation of grammatical rules and the practice of the rules in converting one sentence into another. Many times the practice is done mechanically.

For example, in teaching the passive voice, the rules regarding the conversion of an active sentence into the passive are given and the student mechanically applies those rules. Consider the following two sentences.

Shakespeare wrote *Hamlet*.

Hamlet was written by Shakespeare.

Most students can convert the first sentence into the second correctly, but they are unaware of the fact that there is some difference between the two sentences and that they are appropriate in two different contexts. Students get the impression due to the mechanical exercise that the two sentences mean exactly the same and that it does not matter whether we use the active sentence or the passive sentence. It must be understood, however, that the first sentence is more appropriate in an essay on Shakespeare, whereas the second sentence is more appropriate in an essay on *Hamlet*.

A teacher of English needs to highlight the contexts in which a particular structure is frequently used so that students will be able to use particular structures in appropriate contexts.

Integration of Grammar with Other Areas

Grammar must not be taught in isolation and for its own sake. It is a bad policy to teach grammar only on a particular day of the week. In fact, grammar can be taught while teaching a prose lesson, story-writing or even a poem. It is desirable to teach grammatical points relevant to the other activities going on in the classroom. Topics for composition which involve the use of particular grammatical points can be taken up. For example, the simple present tense can be reinforced through a topic like 'My Daily Routine' and the present continuous tense can be reinforced by asking a student to look out of the window and describe what is happening outside. Students can be given practice in the use of the passive voice through a paragraph on 'How are bicycle punctures repaired?' Because of the enjoyment associated with such topics, students will be able to learn grammar better.

Use of Minimum Technical Terminology

Students are not expected to be experts in the theory of grammar and they need not really know technical terminology used in grammar books and definitions of the technical terms. What is more important is that they should be able to use the language correctly and appropriately. It does not really matter if the students do not know technical terms like infinitive, subjunctive mood, imperative sentence, present perfect continuous tense and assertive sentence. In some cases, the teacher can simplify technical terms and use non-technical terms which are easier to understand. For example, the term 'infinitive' can be replaced by the 'to' form of the verb as in *to see, to run, to go* etc. The term 'past participle' may be replaced by 'the third form of the verb'.

Other Techniques of Simplification

A teacher must be able to make even the weakest student in the class understand his explanation and he can use various strategies for this purpose. Drawing pictures and diagrams is a very useful strategy, because even weak students can understand them without any verbal explanation. Consider how basic uses of prepositions can be taught using the following diagrams indicating the position of objects. Consider the following examples illustrating the use of prepositions to indicate different positions of objects.

- The ball is *on* the table.
- There is a calendar *over* the fire place.
- There is one chair *in* the room.
- He brought one chair *into* the room.

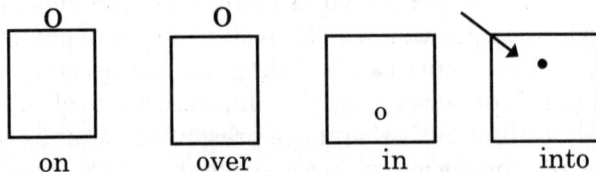

Consider the following examples indicating the use of the past perfect tense and the simple past tense in the same sentence.

She had watched the film before she read the novel.

I had completed my education before I got my first job.

The following diagram simplifies the use of the two tense forms for the students:

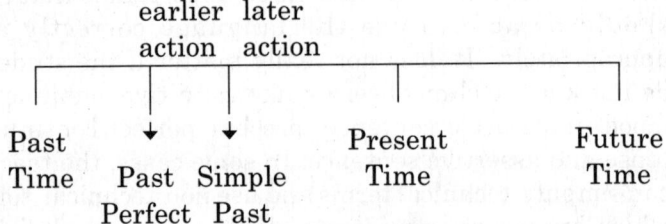

To teach the use of the present continuous tense and the past continuous tense, we often give examples like the following:

My friend is waiting at the bus-stop (now).

She was watching television at 7 p.m. yesterday. The present continuous tense refers to an action which is going on right now, whereas the past continuous tense refers to an action which was incomplete at a point of time in the past. The difference between the present continuous tense and the past continuous tense can be clarified by the following diagrams.

Present Continuous Tense

```
        ↱
├───────┼───────────┤
Past    Present     Future
Time    Time        Time
```

Past Continuous Tense

```
  ↱
├──┼────────┼───────┤
Past    Present     Future
Time    Time        Time
```

Grammar can also be taught effectively through language games. As it is well-known, there are four main patterns of tense sequence in conditional sentences. The class can be divided into two groups. One group may be asked to specify a conditional clause and the other group may be asked to supplement that by a superordinate clause. A lot of unexpected and interesting sentences will be the result of this game and both teachers and students will be able to enjoy it. A considerable amount of learning takes place through such games.

Conclusion

Grammar must not be taught for its own sake. The purpose of the teaching of grammar must be to enable students to use the language effectively and efficiently. The teacher needs to think constantly about how the teaching of grammar can be made simpler and enjoyable. 'Enjoyment is all' in the teaching and learning of English!

11

Teaching of Grammar and Vocabulary

*Simon G. Bernabas**

Introduction

The teaching of English grammar and vocabulary has received a great deal of attention from ELT experts across the world. We have taught English in our country for nearly 200 years. We have happily borrowed the methods and techniques of teaching the language and have engaged in scholarly discussions on the importance of their application in our classrooms. Consequently, our textbooks have contained units/lessons based on the principles of the grammar translation method, structural approach and communicative approach. In spite of our adherence to and application of these approaches many of our reputed teachers of English have indicated that the whole exercise of English teaching in our country has been futile. Consider, for example, these words of Nagarajan(1978): "The English language in India has been…steadily declining for a long while, but we are resolved to let it neither die nor flourish"(161). He adds: "The decline of English in India began soon after its introduction into our universities"(161). Similarly, two veteran professors of English have given this interesting title to the third chapter of their well-known book *English Teaching in India*: "The Story of English Teaching in India: A Tragic Tale"(43). The words and the title indirectly suggest our learners' lack of proficiency in the

---

*****Simon G. Bernabas** is M.A., Ph.D. from Pune University and PGDES and M.Litt. from the CIEFL, Hyderabad. He is a Reader in the PG Dept. of English at Ahmednagar College. His areas of interest are ELLT, English Studies in India and American Literature. He is co-author of *Conversational English* (2010).

skills of the language. My purpose here is not to criticize the methods or techniques employed in our country from time to time, for, as tried and tested procedures, they have their own value. However, we can not overlook the fact that most of us are reluctant to make use of them in our classrooms, particularly with regard to the teaching of grammar and vocabulary. Indeed there are reasons for the poor teaching of the two items. The chief reason is the lack of time. The lack of competent teachers is another serious problem. The governments' insistence on compulsory promotion of all students till Class X makes teachers complacent. Finally, the different proficiency levels of our students in English create a sense of futility in teachers. This is a time when we speak a lot about the teacher's role as a facilitator. Of course, she can successfully assume that role if all her students' proficiency in English is the same. Since that is not the case in most of our institutions, I feel that while teaching grammar and vocabulary to their students, teachers need to *explain* quite a lot even as they attempt to employ the various techniques recommended by experts. Techniques and the teacher's explanation have a complementary role to perform in an ESL classroom of our country.

Teaching of Grammar

Opinions concerning the teaching of grammar vary considerably. The clash of opinions, as the well-known ELT expert Tickoo(2003) points out, is "between those who consider the time spent on grammar teaching as time wasted and those who advocate a full-scale teaching of grammar from early on in any organized course of teaching"(163). Whatever may be the argument, the fact remains that most students feel the necessity of learning grammar because of their faith in the relationship between grammar and correctness. What we teachers need to do in our classrooms is to exploit the belief and make use of some of the tried and tested techniques of teaching English grammar. One of the first things that a college teacher of grammar should do is to spend a few hours on orientation. That is, in a mixed ability class she should assume that her students' level of competence in the four skills of the language couldn't be the same. At this stage she should spend some time explaining the important grammatical concepts such as the parts of speech, tense and articles. She can then test their comprehension by asking them to identify those elements in short passages. The next task of the teacher in a bilingual class is to convince her learners that the grammar of English does not differ considerably from that of their own language: many of the grammatical concepts in English exist in their L1 too. Consider, for example, these concepts and their equivalents: noun (*naam*), adjective (*visheshan*), adverb (*kriyavisheshan*), verb (*kriya*), transitive verb (*sakarmak kriya*), intransitive verb (*akarmak kriya*) and tense (*kaal*). Teaching English through parallel concepts chosen from the mother tongue/ L1 of the learners is a technique that has been discussed by experts.

Tickoo explains the advantage of using the learners' mother tongue thus: "The truth...is that far from being a source of interference or obstruction the learner's mother tongue can become a resource of immense potential"(175). A careful introduction to English grammar through the grammar of their own mother tongue will at least dispel the learners' fear that the grammar they are going to learn is a totally alien system of rules. Of course, I do not presume that teaching parallel concepts poses no problems at all. These parallels need to be explained for clarity and for comparing the features of the two languages. An illustrative example may be given here.

The uses of English tense forms often appear difficult for our students. But many of the uses have their parallels in many Indian languages. An example is the use of the present continuous tense in English and Hindi. Note that each use of the tense in English has its exact parallels in Hindi. The uses[1] are:

a) to denote an action that is in progress at the time of speaking.

For example. The girl is playing = *Ladki khel rahi hai*

b) to describe an action that is in progress and will be continued, but is not necessarily going on at the moment of speaking.

For example. A: What are you doing these days? = *Aaj kal aap kya kar rahen hain?*

B: Well, I am writing a novel = *Main ek novel likh rahan hoon.*

c) to express an action that has been arranged to take place in the near future.

For example. I am going to Mumbai tomorrow = *Main kal Mumbai ja raha hoon.*

Such parallels of some other tenses are also found in Indian languages. However, mother tongue equivalents should not be used extensively because there are certain concepts in English for which such parallels are hard to find. Prepositions and articles are two cases in point. And in some other cases, like the active and passive voices, the change in the order of words can be confusing. Many ELT experts believe that a learner should be aware of the rules of grammar. Penny Ur,(1988) for example, says:" There is no doubt that a knowledge—implicit or explicit—of grammatical rules is essential for the mastery of a language: you cannot use words unless you know how they should be put together"(4). Similarly, Tickoo points out: "...grammar has an important place in one's knowledge of a second or foreign language. It can provide a sound knowledge of usable rules, especially when teaching focuses on aspects of grammar that constitute the basic building blocks of the language"(165).

However, most of the time, despite innovative textbooks, we tend to focus on rules alone with a minimum number of illustrations. Introducing grammatical forms through dialogues/conversations seems to be a fruitful exercise. Fortunately, in recent years, many universities have included units of conversation in their Compulsory English textbooks at the undergraduate level. The units attempt to help learners respond appropriately to different situations. The titles of these units are self- explanatory: introducing oneself, agreeing and disagreeing, joining a conversation, asking for information, accepting/declining an invitation, etc.

These units can be used for improving the learners' spoken and written skills in English. The learners can form small groups to enact the conversations in the class. Their focus on the lines of dialogue will be greater if a healthy competition in terms of playing roles develops among the groups. And because the units are usually short, most of the groups can act their parts in one period.

While acting, the learners are naturally introduced to the expressions useful in the context and they understand how they vary in informal and in formal situations (for example, *I was just wondering if you would come over for dinner tonight* or *How about coming for dinner tonight?*). In the next class the teacher can explain a similar context, for the same expressions. Based on the context, each group may be asked to write a dialogue/conversation in 10 to15 minutes. She can quickly go through their draft dialogues and draw their attention to the necessary corrections to be made. The learners are likely to show more enthusiasm in enacting their own scripts. The repeated use of the expressions in similar contexts can reinforce understanding. In the third stage learners may be allowed to invent a similar situation and write the dialogue themselves. A random checking of their scripts may confirm their understanding of the expressions. Taking the learners from controlled to free acting and writing, it is hoped, will help them discover the grammaticality and acceptability of the expressions. What a teacher is expected to do with such units is to exploit the learners' commonly perceived eagerness to learn spoken English. The advantage of this exercise is that it includes both spoken and written language.

Group discussions can be used as a means in the class to teach other polite conversational expressions, especially those used while agreeing or disagreeing with somebody, and sentence connectors such as **however, therefore, further.** At the initial stage, discussion should be a controlled activity. The teacher may give an idea of the appropriate expressions the participants have to use during the discussion. Gradually, the learners may be given parallel issues for discussion and with much less interventions of the teacher. However, at the end of each discussion she must explain the appropriateness of the expressions, like the following, in informal and formal contexts:

> I am sorry, I can't agree with you.
> I can't say that I share your opinion.
> That's exactly my view.
> Absolutely.

The students' knowledge of these expressions may be reinforced further with exercises like the ones given below:

1) Hamid: The film was really good. What do you think?

Hari: _____ (Write an appropriate expression of agreement/disagreement).

2) Participant 1(in a group discussion): Cricket matches should be banned in India.

Participant 2: _____ (Write an expression of disagreement).

Pictures showing various events and objects may be used to teach structures in lower classes. They may also be useful in higher classes in enhancing the learners' ability to describe events. Basic sentence patterns like there+be+subject may be taught:

There is a hill in the picture.
There are two girls near the well.

If the picture is of a village, for example, students can be asked to consider it as 'my village' and describe it. They may then be asked to describe their original village and describe the differences between the two. Certainly, in the typical Indian classroom the teacher can expect a lot of grammatical errors but what is important is making learners speak the language. Further, the occurrence of errors provides the teacher opportunities to deal with them for the benefit of the whole class.

Pictures can also be used to teach other grammatical items such as the comparison of adjectives. A picture with different objects of varying sizes and qualities may be shown and the learners may be asked to compare the objects. For example, one may say *The tree near the wall is shorter than the other tree* or *The grass on the ground is greener than the leaves of the tree.*

Stories are useful sources in the grammar class. They are often told in the past tense and occasionally, in the present tense. Hence they may be used for the teaching of these two tenses. The story chosen for a class should be interesting and unknown to the students. The teacher may narrate it but she can stop towards the end and ask the learners to complete it without changing the tense (Of course the assumption is that the teacher has already introduced her learners to the tense). The advantage here is that a tale can have different endings depending on the imagination of the learners. Alternatively, the teacher may stop at the various turning points of the story and ask them to say what will happen next. Again, the teacher has to pay attention to their use of the tenses. From stories the teacher may shift the learners' attention to describing past events using the past tense forms. The learners can rewrite the story with their own endings or by writing down their description of events.

Although it is an old form of exercise, rearranging jumbled words to form grammatically meaningful sentences continues to interest learners of all classes. The exercise can be presented in varying degrees of complexity. Thus the teacher may test them by rearranging simple sentences and at advanced levels she may give even paragraphs and passages. In paragraphs the order of the sentences may also be jumbled up to test their ability to follow the principles of discourse analysis.

The techniques described above are simple and selective but their usefulness becomes evident when we introduce them after a certain amount of teaching. Any technique that a teacher employs in the classroom should have the backing of her explanation of the language item(s) she intends to teach via that technique. As has already been pointed out, the teachers' explanation and the techniques have a complementary role to perform in a typical classroom in our country.

Teaching of Vocabulary

One of the areas in English language teaching that has not received much attention in our classrooms is the teaching of vocabulary. The general approach to the teaching of words is rather casual. At least some of us do not seem to focus on the precise meanings of words, phrases and idioms. What we often do is to give a vague or imprecise explanation of difficult words in the students' own mother tongue or in English. This points to the fact that sometimes teachers themselves are not sure of the exact meanings. Many of them seem to loathe the idea of consulting standard dictionaries for meanings and uses. Some teachers guess meanings of words in the classroom while teaching lessons. Although guessing and inferring meanings are two techniques of vocabulary study, their frequent and indiscriminate use in the classroom is dangerous. Further, some consider the various usages of words irrelevant to the immediate purpose of teaching. The result of all these is the students' faulty understanding of words and their meanings.

According to Wallace(1982), some of the symptoms of poor vocabulary learning and/or teaching are: inability to retrieve vocabulary that has been taught, use of vocabulary inappropriate to the given situation, use of vocabulary at the wrong level of formality, possessing the wrong kind of vocabulary for one's needs, using vocabulary in an unidiomatic way, using vocabulary in a meaningless way, incorrect use of dictionary and use of incorrect grammatical form, spelling, pronunciation, or stress.[2] . Tickoo has usefully explained what word study actually means(191). In a typical classroom a teacher may not be able to focus her attention on all those aspects of vocabulary learning, that too in 35 to 45 minutes. However, she can devote a couple of periods at the beginning of the year to train the students in using a good monolingual and bilingual dictionary, keeping in mind the different aspects of word study. This 'orientation program' can save a lot of time in the subsequent classes.

As a teacher of English, I have not come across any class that has not shown a sincere interest in vocabulary study. In fact most of them believe, wrongly, of course, that using grandiloquent words in speaking and writing is a sign of good knowledge of the language. This belief has to be corrected but we also must exploit their enthusiasm and help them use the right word in the right place, both in writing and speaking. In this regard we have to depend on the vocabulary items given in each textbook, which are normally found in selections like *A General Service List of English Words* (Michael West) or the 'Oxford 3000'[3] .

One of the simplest and traditional techniques of vocabulary teaching is to explain word meanings in contexts. The primary duty of the teacher is to give a very clear and precise definition of the word in question. To begin with, the illustration of the word can be done through very short dialogues prepared by the teacher herself. Consider, for example, the word *appointment*. The common meaning of the word, as 'a job or position of responsibility', may be known to the students but the meaning to be taught here is: 'an arrangement to meet someone or do something at a particular time'. After mentioning this meaning of the word the teacher should reinforce its use with a short dialogue like the following:

Rahul: Wasim, why don't you have dinner with me today?

Wasim: Sorry, Rahul, I have an appointment with my doctor in the evening.

She may now seek similar examples from the learners.

As far as possible, students should be introduced to other important and useful meanings of the same word. This point can be illustrated with the help of the following two meanings of the word *endorse*:

i) to say publicly that you support a person, statement or an action.

This meaning may be the intended meaning in the textbook/unit and it can be introduced by providing a suitable context like the one described above. But the teacher should also draw their attention to the second meaning that has special relevance in this age of advertisements:

ii) to say in an advertisement that you like and use a particular product

(For example, a shaving cream)

Ramesh: I understand that the popular actor Rupesh Kumar has agreed to endorse a shaving cream produced by an obscure company.

Paul: It seems that the company has offered him a huge sum of money for its endorsement.

If time permits the teacher can give one-line sentences like the following to illustrate the above meanings further:

I fully endorse everything that the captain of our team has said.

Companies pay thousands of rupees to actors to endorse their new product on the TV.

There are many other techniques that a teacher can effectively use in the classroom for teaching vocabulary. One of the techniques is the use of translation equivalents. But this simple technique, as in the case of teaching grammar, should not be misused. Frequent explanation of word meanings in the learners' L1 may divert their attention from the target language, that is, English. Similarly, if the class comprises learners of different linguistic backgrounds then the technique might not work. Hence it is advisable to give meanings first in the target language itself and then their equivalents in the LI, if necessary. However, finding the equivalents can be turned into an interesting exercise.

She can ask her students to find the equivalents by referring to a good bilingual dictionary.

The learners may be asked to keep their own wordbook containing the meanings of English words in LI. The teacher may occasionally go through the book to encourage them. She may also give a select list of terms pertaining to specific fields/registers such as science and technology, governance or religion. This is especially useful because translations of all kinds of works are welcome now and many official application forms are in the local language of the applicants. Further, the exercise can introduce learners to the features of registral variations of their own languages.

There are certain simpler techniques that may prove useful in lower classes. The use of actual objects can be helpful in getting the meaning engraved in the learners' minds. The various tools used by artisans/ mechanics or the cutlery used in the kitchen, can be shown to the students. However, it may be inconvenient for the teacher to carry such items to class and take them away regularly. That is where pictures and drawings come in handy. These aids may be used for obtaining a clear idea of the objects/items in question. It is a fact that a large number of our college students do not know the difference between a 'toe' and a 'finger'; the two words are often used synonymously. Even postgraduates are unable to name certain parts of the human body like the knuckle, cuticle, shin, instep, sole, etc. Good dictionaries like the *Oxford Advanced Learner's Dictionary* have neatly labeled diagrams of the body in them and an enthusiastic teacher can use the enlarged copies of these diagrams in the classroom to teach the various parts. Such dictionaries also contain other diagrams/pictures showing the parts of, say, a house, car or aircraft. A good teacher is a good collector of pictures. Pictures can be used to teach not only nouns but also actions and moods.

Two items that have special relevance to vocabulary teaching are collocations and phrasal verbs. Unfortunately, both these items have received scant attention from our teachers. The right use of collocations can make learners' speech natural and pleasing. It will be better if the teacher identifies the most useful collocations used in a textbook and pay special attention to them while teaching each unit in her class. According to McCarthy and O'Dell (2002), learning collocations has important uses for the learners. Collocations can give them the most natural way to say something and give them alternative ways of saying something in a style of writing(6).Teachers must emphasize the importance of collocations and right at the beginning of the course they must train their learners to identify collocations. They need to stop awhile to explain the use of collocations in the context of each lesson. For instance, a teacher who teaches Chinua Achebe's *Things Fall Apart*(1958) to an undergraduate class can draw her learners' attention to certain fine uses of collocation. In Chapter 19 of the novel, the pulling out of a tuber is described thus: "They just pulled the stump, and the earth rose, roots snapped below, and the tuber was pulled out" *(150)*. The perceptive teacher will immediately notice the special relevance of the collocations in the sentence to the 'agrarian' Indian classroom. She may draw their attention to: *pull a stump, earth rises, roots snap* and *pull out a tuber.*

Many interesting exercises in collocations can be given to a class. They may be done either in school/college or at home. One exercise is matching the items in collocations:

mass	drugs
broad	appeal
take	of memory
lapse	minded

A second kind of exercise is the identification of wrong collocations in a short paragraph: when the poor young boy did suicide the entire village fell sad. The villagers made everything possible to lend him an attractive burial. So they ordered money from everyone.

A third kind is completing questions with a list of words given:

(massive, radical, campus, curiosity)
Does the principal stay on the college ———————?
Can the teacher arouse her students'——————— ?
Was the heart attack ———————?
Is he a ——————— politician?

In fact, books on collocations contain a large number of exercises for the teacher to choose from. All that is to be done is to make use of them for the benefit of the students. As mentioned earlier, phrasal verbs as a teaching item also deserves special attention on part of the teacher. Cowie and Mackin(1993) say: "Phrasal verbs are commonly used by native speakers but constitute a well-known stumbling block for foreign learners, who because of the associated problems of structure or meaning may fall back on a more formal one-word equivalent"(422). The first step in teaching phrasal verbs is to give a general introduction to their form and the occurrences of their constituent elements in sentences. Similarly, as in the case of collocations, the teacher should be very selective while looking for phrasal verbs for her class. There seems to be a widespread belief that teaching all the phrasal verbs under a headword consecutively will be useful. However, it is better to remember that teaching a succession of them, under one keyword, will only confuse the learners and confusing the elements in phrasal verbs, obviously, can have adverse denotational consequences. Hence, selecting the most frequently used ones for teaching will be a good idea and, as McCarthy and O'Dell say, "The best way to learn phrasal verbs is undoubtedly in context"(204). Two examples are discussed here, under the keyword *ask*, to illustrate the selection and contextual teaching of phrasal verbs.

a) *ask after* = ask for news of

Rahul: I met our high school friend Majid at a party yesterday.

Rohan: Really? I wish I too were there.

Rahul: Yes. Anyway, he has asked after you and your mother.

b) *ask in* = invite someone to enter the house.

Thomas: Our uncle seemed to be in a foul mood yesterday.

Jacob: Why? What happened?

Thomas: I went to wish him a happy birthday but he didn't even ask me in; he kept me standing at the door.

Indeed there are other phrasal verbs with *ask* but for Indian students the above two, I think, are more useful since they use the more formal *enquire about* and *invite me inside* in the above examples. The advantage is that the teacher can teach these phrasal verbs when the word *ask* occurs somewhere in the textbook. Certainly, after a certain gap of time the learners may be introduced to the other related expressions like *ask out* or *ask for*. Some other useful phrasal verbs that can be taught this way are: *answer back, boil away, boil over, catch up with, get on,* etc. The teacher should be very sensitive to the utility of such items. Fortunately, the headwords of most phrasal verbs regularly appear in textbooks.

Other simple exercises also can be used in the classroom to teach phrasal verbs. For instance, a set of incomplete statements containing a headword can be given and students may be asked to complete them with its other particles (adverb/preposition). Some examples, containing *turn* as the key word, are given below:

I applied to the party for membership but my application was turned―――――.

When he left my house the cook forgot to turn――――― the gas stove.

I waited for my friend for a long time but he didn't turn ―――――.

Of course, when in doubt the learners can consult a dictionary. Another exercise can be a passage or a set of sentences containing some phrasal verbs, which may be underlined. The students should describe their meanings in the context of the passage/sentences. For example:

Nikhil and Habib were great pals. Their friends saw them together all the time. In times of difficulty they *backed up* each other. Their honesty was famous in their town and it was *borne out* by one and all. They were prompt in *carrying out* their duties. However, after their SSC, they had to leave for two different cities for higher education. The parting was painful, but they *put up* with it. They *got on* very well at their colleges and when they met after 6 months they had so much to talk about.

Asking learners to use select phrasal verbs contextually, especially in short dialogues, is another useful exercise.

For teaching general vocabulary items, too, the teacher can employ certain useful exercises. Rewriting sentences, without changing their meaning and using a specific word given in brackets, is one such exercise. An example is given below:

My friend has the habit of judging people and criticizing them too quickly.

(Judgmental)

A list of verbs and their meanings can be given first and learners may be asked to fill in gaps in sentences with the appropriate forms of the verbs. Here is an example

Verbs:

to retool = to replace or change the machine or equipment in a factory.

to mend = to repair something.

Sentences:

When workers went on strike frequently Mr. Menon shifted his factory to Madurai and ——————— it.

My shoes were in a bad shape. A cobbler ——————— them for me.

Nouns denoting peculiar habits of people or qualities of objects may be presented thus:

What do we call
a) a man who hates women?
b) a person who draws maps?
c) an instrument that is used to measure temperature?

Conclusion

In the foregoing pages an attempt has been made to explain certain techniques that can be used in the ESL classroom to teach grammar and vocabulary. Indeed they are not at all new techniques. What is emphasized here, with some simple illustrations, is that their appropriate use in the classroom can make our attempts to teach grammar and vocabulary more effective and success-oriented.

Notes

1. The uses of the Tenses have been summarized from Tickoo *et al* : 107-38.
2. Summarized from Wallace: 8 -13.
3. Hornby, H. S (2005) *Oxford Advanced Learner's Dictionary.* Seventh edn. Oxford: OUP. 'Oxford 3000' is given in the Reference Section (R): 97-111.

References

1. Achebe, C (1958). *Things Fall Apart.* rpt 2004. Mumbai: Allied Publishers Pvt. Ltd.
2. Cowie, A. P and Mackin, R (1993). *Oxford Dictionary of Phrasal Verbs.* Oxford:OUP.
3. Krishnaswamy, N and Sriraman, T(1994) *English Teaching in India.* Madras: TR Publications.
4. Mc Carthy, M and O'Dell (2002) *English Vocabulary in Use.* Cambridge:CUP.
5. Nagarajan, S (1978) 'The Decline of English in India' in M. Manual, and K. Ayyappa Panikar (Eds*) English in India.* 161-171.
6. Tickoo, M.L (2003) *Teaching and Learning: A Sourcebook for Teachers and Trainers.* Hyderabad: Orient Longman.
7. Tickoo, M.L, Subramanian, A.E and Subramanian, P. R (1976). *Intermediate Grammar,*
   Usage and Composition. Hyderabad: Orient Longman.
8. Ur, P (1988). *Grammar Practice Activities: A Practical Guide for Teachers.* Cambridge: CUP.
9. Wallace, M.J (1982). *Teaching Vocabulary.* London: Heinemann Educational Books.

12 Enriching Vocabulary
Shirin Shaikh

Importance of Vocabulary

Sound, structure, meaning and vocabulary are four important constituents of language teaching. All these constituents hold an equal place of importance, but according to Morris (1969), 'Viewed in the right perspective as a concomitant feature of the language abilities, vocabulary is unquestionably a major consideration' (29). It is impossible to learn a language without learning the vocabulary of that language. Vocabulary is considered important because if one wants to frame single sentences, one needs a stock of vocabulary. Our competence in using any language depends on the number of words we know in that language. The more words we know, the more competent we are in the use of a language Tickoo (2003) remarks, 'True mastery of a language lies as much in knowing and appropriately using its vocabulary as in being able to use its system of sounds and its grammatical and discoursal patterns' (189). We can explore and analyse the world around us with the help of words. Regarding the importance of vocabulary Spender (1980) remarks, 'In order to live in the world, we must name it. Names are essential for the construction of reality for without a name it is difficult to accept the existence of an object, an event, a feeling. Naming is the means whereby we attempt to order and

---

*****Shirin Shaikh.** Ph.D. is a lecturer in English at the Poona College of Arts, Science and Commerce, Pune. She has published several articles in national and international journals. An experienced teacher and trainer at the undergraduate and post-graduate levels, Dr. Shaikh's interests include linguistics and English language teaching.

structure the chaos and flux of existence which would otherwise be an undifferentiated mass. By assigning names we impose a pattern and a meaning which allows us to manipulate the world' (163).

Learning new words expands our understanding and improves our mind. Every new word that is learnt entices our mind to stretch itself into new areas. We can improve our ability to think and express ourselves in a better way with the help of larger vocabulary. In today's world, the ability to use words effectively is often highly rewarded. One can understand the exact meaning of what he hears and reads if one has adequate vocabulary and so there is no misunderstanding on his part. Adequate knowledge of vocabulary allows one to speak and write easily and fluently. It makes his speech and writing vivid, effective and interesting. It enables the speaker to adopt the correct tone to suit the audience and purpose. It gives pleasure to the audience. It provides a range of precise words to use in appropriate context. It enables one to convey the shades of meaning and colour which are particularly useful in creative or narrative writing.

Teaching of Vocabulary to Undergraduate Students

At the primary level, more attention should be paid to grammatical and phonological accuracy and vocabulary may be restricted to a few words, but in higher classes it is important to enrich the students' vocabulary. The students at the undergraduate level are in a better position to enlarge their vocabulary because at this level the students know the sound system, the sentence patterns and common words reasonably well.

The teacher should also create word-consciousness among the students at this level.

In the general teaching programme followed in the Indian colleges at the undergraduate level, teachers find it difficult to teach important words systematically. Most teachers generally provide the meanings of useful words and assume that their work of teaching vocabulary is accomplished. Providing the learners with only the meanings of words is not a very effective method of teaching vocabulary. In this way the learners do not learn new words and they do not use the language with accuracy, precision and appropriateness. Therefore, the teacher must be very careful while teaching the students important vocabulary items. The teacher must bring in other vocabulary items which are close to the target words. Similarly, the teacher should show the fine distinctions between the semantically related words with regards to the meaning and usage. The teacher must introduce the words, in a way that the learners understand the meaning of the words more precisely and become effective users of the language.

The Students' Problems

At the undergraduate level, most of the students know the basic grammar of the language and so they generally manage to communicate well without making major grammatical mistakes but their stock of vocabulary is often inadequate. Since they have not acquired an adequate stock of vocabulary, they overuse some general words which makes their discourse sound weak and they fail to convey different moods or connotations. They are unable to communicate the intended message precisely. They need to expand their vocabulary in order to express themselves more clearly and appropriately in a wide range of situations.

A majority of undergraduate learners can recognize the words and their meanings but their productive use of vocabulary is often limited. This problem arises because the students' active English vocabulary is made up almost entirely of common words that are the simplest and most frequently occurring words in English. It is definitely important to learn the common words before the rare ones but often these words get deeply rooted in the learners' lexicon and it becomes difficult to replace these common words with the words that have a more specific meaning.

Thus, generally students at the undergraduate level have a superficial knowledge of vocabulary. They need a deeper and conceptual understanding of words. They cannot just learn vocabulary at a deeper or conceptual level just by reading or by definitions. Word knowledge is complex and consists of more than knowing meaning. Knowing a word involves knowing several aspects of vocabulary. It is important that the teachers deal with these aspects when teaching vocabulary.

Aspects of Vocabulary

Vocabulary cannot be regarded as simple accumulation of isolated word meanings. Any word is a part of a larger, indeterminate set of words. In order to understand the word precisely it is important to understand the complex inter-relationship that exists between the words of the same lexical set. Teaching vocabulary involves teaching the various aspects of vocabulary. Some of the aspects are as follows:

Aspects of Vocabulary

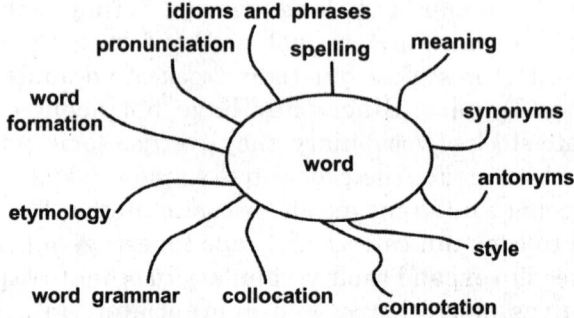

1. Pronunciation

Pronunciation is one of the important aspects of vocabulary. Students should be able to recognize the word when they hear it and they should also be able to produce the correct spoken form in order to express themselves. Lexical knowledge of second language learners is useless unless they are able to make themselves intelligible when they speak. Similarly, unfamiliarity with correct pronunciation can result in students' failure to understand certain words in connected speech. Therefore, teaching pronunciation is an essential part of teaching vocabulary if the new lexical items are to be used effectively and understood without difficulty.

Pronunciation is problematic for the learners of English because there is often no clear relation between the written form of a word (spelling) and its pronunciation (sound). Due to the arbitrariness of English spellings and sounds, the learners find it difficult to master these aspects of lexical items.

Every language allows certain combinations of sound and disallows certain others. It is important that the teachers seek out the regularities that give the students confidence in dealing with the pronunciation of new vocabulary.

Students can predict the silent letters in pronunciation from the spelling patterns. For example, 'k' is silent in words that begin with 'kn' such as 'knee', 'knead', 'knife', 'knew', 'knit', 'knock' and 'knight'. Similarly, 'b' is silent at the end of words that are preceded by 'm', for example, 'comb', 'dumb', 'plumb' and 'tomb'. Teachers should provide the students with some general guidelines in order to help them to predict the pronunciation of new lexical items. Spelling patterns which usually conform to a particular pronunciation should be pointed out to the students. For example, the letters 'au' generally represent the sound / ɔː/ as in the words 'caught' and 'taught'. This will help them to gain better pronunciation.

In order to pronounce words correctly the students should be able to produce the spoken form of a word and be able to stress the appropriate syllable of the word if it contains more than one syllable. In the following words different syllables are stressed.

a) politics /ˈpɒlɪtɪks /

b) political /pəˈlɪtɪkəl/

c) politician /ˌpɒlɪˈtɪʃən/

Thus the stress shift from one syllable to a different syllable produces a different vowel. This influence on different syllables makes correct stress such an important factor in being intelligible. For example, in the word 'police' the second syllable is stressed and so it is pronounced as /pəˈliːs / but learners who stress the first syllable of 'police' will pronounce the word as /ˈpɒlis/. Due to inappropriate stress they may not be understood.

The learners of English as a second or foreign language find it difficult to master pronunciation because of the lack of consistency between spelling and pronunciation. A rudimentary knowledge of phonemic symbols can greatly assist the students by providing access to the pronunciation of new words. This gives the students an opportunity to work independently and they do not need the teacher constantly as an intermediary. The knowledge of phonemic symbols certainly provides guidance to the students in order to enable them to approximate the sound to a point where they are at least intelligible.

When the new word is introduced in the class, the teacher should write the new word on the blackboard and also write the phonemic transcription and indicate the primary stress if the word has more than one syllable. There are two advantages of having the phonemic transcription on the board. Firstly, it acts as a reminder to the students not to be misled by the spelling (orthographic form) and secondly, phonemic symbols and stress markers provide valuable visual assistance to the learners who are not very good listeners and who cannot imitate the English sounds orally from the model provided by the teacher. It is easier for the students to grasp both sound and stress patterns by seeing them represented graphically.

2. *Spelling*

Spelling is the graphic form of a word. As mentioned earlier, the spelling of English words cannot always be inferred from their pronunciation because English spelling is in part conventional. The irregularity in the English spelling system creates difficulty for the learners of English. The learners' writing skill can be affected due to poor spelling. The learners may use limited vocabulary by avoiding words that are hard to spell and selecting regularly spelled words. Therefore, the teacher should concentrate on spelling while teaching vocabulary. When introducing a new word, the teacher should write down the spelling of the new word on the blackboard. Relating the spoken form of a word to its written form can help the students improve their spellings. The teacher should train the students in the use of spelling strategies and encourage the students to become independent in their application.

3. *Meaning*

In teaching vocabulary it is important to get across the meaning of the items clearly and to ensure that the students understand the meaning of the words correctly.

The learners should know the spoken form of the word (pronunciation), the written form of the word (spelling) and they should also know the meaning. Most of the words are polysemous. A word is said to be polysemous if it has two or more meanings. English has many polysemous words. According to linguists like Bollinger and Sears (1981), it is out of economy that polysemy exists in language. It is possible to get along with a few words by using them in patterns of repetition and combination. For example, the word 'head' could mean 'part of our body', 'top position of a bed', 'in-charge of an institute' or 'top portion of a needle'.

4. Grammar

Teaching grammar is another aspect of teaching vocabulary. Words in a language belong to one or the other grammatical categories. The learners should understand the function that a word performs in a sentence i.e. they should know the grammatical category to which the word belongs.

Providing the learners with grammatical information about a word enables them to build up different forms of words. Similarly, in order to use a word it is necessary to know what part of speech it belongs to and also what grammatical patterns it can fit into. The knowledge of word grammar as well as sentence grammar helps the students to use the same word in more than one category.

5. Word Formation

The knowledge of the processes of word formation can help the students to expand their vocabulary. The strategies of word formation help the students both productively and receptively. In terms of productive skills, the knowledge of the principles of word building can help the students to widen their range of expression. In terms of receptive skills, knowledge or understanding of the processes of word building can help the learners to guess the meaning of unknown items. It is necessary to teach the learners the processes of word formation in order to show the relatedness of words. The students at the undergraduate level already know some words. With the help of the processes of word formation, the new words related to the known word class can be easily understood by the students.

6. Collocation

Collocation is another important aspect of vocabulary. The term 'collocation' is used to refer to two or more words that commonly occur together. When words occur together regularly, rules are formed about their use, not for grammatical reasons but because of association. For example, the words 'black and white' appear in that order because of collocation and to put them the other way round seems wrong. Consider the following sentences.

a) Jim *badly wanted* the police to leave.
b) Jim *badly wished* the police to leave.
c) Jim *earnestly wanted* the police to leave.
d) Jim *earnestly wished* the police to leave.

'Badly' can co-occur with 'wanted' but it cannot co-occur with 'wished'. But 'earnestly' can occur with 'wanted' as well as with 'wished'. An awareness of these patterns of collocation can make the teaching of collocation easier for the teachers. The most common types of collocations are as follows.

a) verb + noun

For example,

(i) Women *commit* fewer *crimes* than men.

The words 'commit' and 'crime' are more likely to occur together.

b) adjective + noun

For example,

(ii) There was *heavy traffic* on the highway.

The words 'heavy' and 'traffic' collocate better than 'big' and 'traffic' or 'intense' and 'traffic'.

An understanding of collocation is vital for all students. It is important to raise students' awareness of collocation as early as possible. Mastery of collocation leads to increase in fluency. The students should be aware of the variety and sheer density of this feature of the language. The teacher through increased exposure can help the students to acquire the knowledge of word collocations.

7. Synonyms

A synonym is a word that means the same as another word or more or less the same. The words are synonymous very rarely on every occasion. Most of the synonyms are partial synonyms. The use of synonyms can be a quick and efficient way of explaining unknown words. The teacher should highlight the subtle differences that exist between the synonymous words. Synonyms can provide the students with words that can express different shades of meaning. For example, for the word 'angry', the students can use more appropriate words like 'annoyed', 'indignant', 'grumpy', 'grouchy', 'infuriated', 'disgusted', 'livid', 'furious', 'exasperated' and 'seething'.

8. Antonyms

The word 'antonym' is used for 'oppositeness' of meaning. Antonymy is often thought of as the opposite of synonymy, but the two have different status. There are three major types of 'oppositeness'. They are as follows.

a) Complementary antonyms which are pairs of words like 'single' and 'married', 'dead' and 'alive', 'animate' and 'inanimate' and 'male' and 'female'. The denial of one word implies the assertion of the other. The sentence 'Smita is not single' implies 'she is married' or 'Smita is not married' implies 'she is single'.

b) Certain pairs of words have another form of 'oppositeness' called **Converse Antonyms**. 'Buy' is the converse of 'sell'. The sentence 'Jack sold his house to John' implies that John bought Jack's house from him. Similarly, the sentence 'The painting is above the fireplace' implies that the fireplace is below the painting. In the above stated examples, the relationship between the pairs of words is reciprocal. Some more examples of converse antonyms are give - receive, come - go, husband - wife.

c) Gradable Antonyms

These are pairs of words like 'big' and 'small', 'young' and 'old', 'tall' and 'short', 'narrow' and 'wide'. The characteristic feature of these antonyms is that they are gradable. The sentences containing gradable antonyms are explicitly or implicitly comparative. For example, 'John's house is big' implies that John's house is bigger than the houses that are normally found. Similarly, when we say 'John's house is small' it implies that John's house is smaller than the houses that are generally found.

9. Style

It is important to create an awareness of different levels of formality as the learners become proficient in a language. Style is an important aspect of vocabulary because even if the learners are reasonably fluent and accurate in a language, errors of style can create misunderstanding without the learner being aware of it. Style may vary according to the written and spoken form of a language. We generally tend to use phrasal verbs and idioms more in spoken English, as compared to written English. The following sentences highlight the difference between formal and informal vocabulary.

i) Jane's telephone has been *disconnected*.

ii) Jane's phone has been *cut off*.

In (i) the word 'disconnect' is more formal than the phrase 'cut off' used in (ii).

iii) They *abolished* the old customs.

iv) They *got rid of* the old customs.

In (iii) the word 'abolished' is more formal than the phrase 'got rid of' used in (iv).

v) Mary was *reprimanded* by her teacher.

vi) Mary was *told off* by her teacher.

In (v) the word 'reprimanded' is more formal than the phrase 'told off' used in (vi).

10. Connotation

The subtle implication or the emotional association that a word carries is called the connotation of a word. Often the connotation of a word is different from its dictionary definition. The words 'house' and 'home' overlap in meaning but they differ in connotation. The word 'house' can be used neutrally but the word 'home' has emotive or attitudinal associations.

Some words have very strong connotation. The teachers should bring the connotation to the notice of the students. Lack of knowledge of the connotation of a word can create problems for the students. For example, both the words 'childish' and 'childlike' mean something like a child but the word 'childish' is used pejoratively, whereas the word 'childlike' is used appreciatively. The knowledge of word connotation definitely helps the students to communicate effectively.

11. Etymology

Etymology is the study of the historical relation between a word and the earlier form or forms from which it has developed. Etymology can help the learners to understand the word better. Etymological information can often be used as a motivation for learning and retention. For example, the word 'photograph' evolved from old Greek words 'photo' meaning light and 'graphikos' meaning writing. The word 'photograph' was first used in English in 1839.

Etymological knowledge can provide learners with meaningful information. This helps the learners to become more sensitive to the meaning of words and their relationship with other words.

a) It can guide the learners to the meaning of unfamiliar words.
b) It can enable the learners to associate one word with other words.
c) It can help the learners to remember words.
d) It can create a greater interest in words and give the learners a clearer insight into their exact shades of meaning.

Therefore, word etymology is definitely a surer and more confident way of mastering vocabulary.

12. Usage

The teacher should not only explain the meanings of the new words but also use the new words in sentences. Every good dictionary provides the usage of the target word. Often examples of word usage in sentences can help the students more than the definition. Sometimes the students may find the meaning of the word a little confusing. So they may misunderstand what the word means. But the sample sentences provided by the teacher can clear all such doubts. Sample sentences also exemplify the grammar of the word and the way the word is used with other words. It becomes easier for the students to form correct sentences with the help of the sample sentences. Providing the students with word usage helps the students to gain confidence in using the words in context. The teachers should have the skill to compose clear and simple example sentences.

13. Phrases

Teaching phrases is an important part of vocabulary teaching at any level but at the undergraduate level, the students can obviously cope with phrases in a better way. At this level the students can explore new meanings of familiar words in phrases like 'the other day' and 'to put up with'. Many phrases consist of words that are individually familiar to the students at this level. From the point of view of learning, this should make such phrases relatively easy to master but the danger is that the students do not consider them as new vocabulary items. Teachers and learners usually focus their attention on individual words that they are unfamiliar with. The knowledge of phrases can definitely enhance the students' expressive power and at the same time help the students become more fluent.

14. Idioms

A sequence of words that operates as a single semantic unit is called an idiom. The meaning of an idiom is not obvious from the meaning of individual words that make up the idiom. For example, the idiom 'to drive somebody round the bend' means 'to make one angry or frustrated' but it is difficult to guess the meaning of the idiom from the individual words. There are syntactic restrictions on the use of idiom. Therefore, most of the idioms are restricted in their form and cannot be changed or varied.

Idioms like 'it is raining cats and dogs' are more immutable. They cannot be transformed into the passive nor do they allow for insertion. For example,
1) It is raining dogs and cats.
2) It is raining cat and dog.
3) It is thundering/pouring cats and dogs.

Idioms present difficulties for the second language learners due to restricted collocations which cannot generally be understood from the literal meaning of the words that make them up. For example, the idiom 'to have cold feet' means 'to be afraid'. This idiom cannot be modified to 'frozen feet' or 'chilly feet' without changing the meaning. Similarly, the idiom 'to let the cat out of the bag' means 'to reveal a secret'. This cannot be decoded from the meaning of the individual words like 'let', 'cat', 'out', 'bag'. But all idioms are not restricted. For example, idioms like 'to drop a brick' means 'to make a mistake'. For this idiom transformation is possible. One can transform this idiom into the passive. For example, 'a brick has been dropped' i.e. a mistake has been made. Insertions, too, are allowed. For example, 'Jim has dropped a really enormous brick this time'. Some idioms are structurally more flexible. For example, the idiom 'to break one's heart' can undergo a wide range of morphological transformations like 'heart-break', 'heart-breaker', 'heart-broken', 'heart-breaking' etc.

Suggestions for Teachers

Most language teachers assume that mastery of the second language depends upon the mastery of syntactic rules. Grammar is certainly a vital component of any language but the mastery of grammatical rules alone cannot help the students attain a higher level of language competence. The knowledge of adequate vocabulary is equally important in the study of a language if one desires to become an effective and impressive communicator. Therefore, it is essential to create awareness among ESL teachers regarding the importance of vocabulary. The following suggestions may be made for the teachers in order to enhance their students' vocabulary.

(a) The teacher should provide the students with a systematic and sustained programme that accelerates the development of vocabulary.

(b) The teacher should help the students expand their passive as well as active vocabulary.

(c) Pronunciation and spelling are important aspects of vocabulary. Therefore, the teacher should see to it that the students pronounce and spell the words properly. The teacher should introduce phonemic transcription in the class in order to improve the students' pronunciation.

(d) Teachers should systematically teach specific roots and affixes. This helps the students to understand better the existing vocabulary.

(e) The stylistic value of vocabulary is considered an essential part of vocabulary teaching and so the teacher should specify whether the word is used in the formal or informal context. Wherever possible the teacher should also provide the students with usage labels like 'slang', 'taboo', 'technical', 'archaic' and 'literary'.

(f) Knowing a word is more than knowing its definition or meaning. The teacher should make use of the most effective and efficient techniques to teach words. Instruction in vocabulary must be rich and multi-faceted. Students must have multiple and varied encounters with words.

(g) Students do not really know a word until they know its collocational profile. Therefore, a teacher should provide the students with collocational information about words.

(h) The teacher should guide the students in deducing the meaning of the unfamiliar words from the contexts in which they are embedded.

(i) The teacher should encourage the students to express their ideas freely with the help of new vocabulary and if necessary correct them in a way that they understand the nature of their errors.

(j) The teacher should motivate the students to learn new words by making vocabulary instruction enjoyable.

(k) The teacher should encourage the students to read and take active part in word games.

(l) The teacher should highlight the benefits of using dictionaries and encourage the students to make maximum use of dictionaries. The teacher should introduce them to dictionaries like *The Longman Dictionary of Contemporary English* and *Oxford Advanced Learner's Dictionary*.

(m) The teacher should evaluate the students' performance and try innovative approaches, including effective use of new technologies and increase the students' learning and confidence.

The teacher can play a major role in helping the learners gain mastery of vocabulary. Teaching of vocabulary requires a variety of strategies, adequate opportunities for exploration and use of the words in meaningful contexts. Unless the teacher is enthusiastic about teaching new words, nothing can help the students learn new vocabulary. A relatively small investment of the time spent on vocabulary activities can have a great impact on the students' knowledge of vocabulary.

References

Bollinger, D. and Sears, D.A. (1981) *Aspects of Languages*. New York: Harcourt Brace Jovanvich Inc.

Morris, I. (1969) *The Art of Teaching English as a Living Language*, London: Macmillan & Co.

Spender, D. (1980) *Man Made Language,* London: Routledge and Kegan Paul.

Thorat, A.; Valke, B. and Gokhale, S.B. (2000) *Enriching Your Competence In English*, Chennai: Orient Longman.

Tickoo, M.L. (2003) *Teaching and Learning English*, New Delhi: Orient Longman Private Limited.

13

Teaching Language to Large Classes

Madhuri Gokhale

Introduction

Teaching is essentially meant to bring about a desirable change in every individual student. It is felt that every student in the class should be able to derive pleasure in the process of learning, and perceive the transformation that has taken place within himself or herself at the end of the year. At the same time, it is very important that for every teacher, teaching proves to be an enjoyable activity and it gives him/her immense satisfaction.

A teacher is expected to accelerate the progress of all students in the class and develop their personality, self-expression and self-confidence. In ancient times, the *Gurukul* system of education was prevalent in India and the disciples used to stay with their teacher during the course of their training in order to gain knowledge. In this system, a teacher was able to give personal attention to every student and a good rapport was established between the teacher and the student. There was no classroom teaching, but knowledge was generally imparted to the students amidst the natural surroundings.

As time passed by, the Gurukul system of education came to an end, and the educational system underwent a significant change. The Industrial Revolution proved to be a turning point in the history of the World and it led to several changes in the educational scenario. The

---

***Madhuri Gokhale** is Asstt. Professor of English at Fergusson College, in English at, Pune. She has M.A, M.Phil. and Ph.D. degrees in English from the University of Pune. She is a recipient of 'The Alegaonkar Brothers Gold Medal'. Her areas of interest are Grammar, ELLT and Stylistics.

University education system started growing and gradually classrooms were formulated on the basis of the students' age group. Educating the poor became one of the major objectives in India, and with the spread of education, classrooms became larger and moved into buildings. Over the years, there has been a rise in the number of students in every class and nowadays at the undergraduate level a compulsory English class typically has around 140 students.

Most of the teachers dealing with compulsory English classes love to talk from 'bell to bell' without wasting a 'single precious minute'. They expect utter silence from the students as they believe in the notion that a quiet environment facilitates learning. Thus, these teachers seem to act like dictators, who do not provide opportunities for any kind of interaction. In most cases, the teacher reads the lesson, gives the meanings of words, analyses the text and dictates notes and thus the teacher seems to be the most active person in the classroom. Naturally, it is monotonous for students to attend such lectures as the only role that they have to play in such classes is that of passive recipients. The consequence is that very often students lose interest in the subject and they start looking upon their studies as a kind of burden rather than a pleasurable activity.

Teaching Compulsory English in Large Classes

It has been argued in several seminars and conferences that the lecturing mode needs to be adopted while dealing with the difficult task of teaching large classes. *Large classes are generally considered to be major impediments to conduct innovative activities in the classroom.* It is true that handling large classes is not easy. However, since they are inevitable aspects of our education system, the better alternative would be to approach the problem of class strength in an optimistic manner rather than letting it come in the way of the students' development and progress. It is felt that if our classrooms are not going to change soon, time has come that we, as teachers, change our teaching strategies.

Large classes would not necessarily be considered obstacles for teaching effectively if the teacher plans the lesson well and plays the role of a facilitator. Good classroom management is a key to success in this kind of situation. It must be remembered that *class control is never a problem for a good teacher who simplifies the subject matter* and makes sure that students understand everything that is taught in the class. An attempt has been made in this article to reveal some of the ways of handling large compulsory English classes.

In a classroom in which only the technique of lecturing is adopted, a teacher often plays the role of a disciplinarian who believes in perfect silence in the classroom. Effective teaching in the classroom does not occur by chance. For effective teaching it is necessary for a teacher to play multiple roles - those of a counsellor, motivator, facilitator and most importantly that of a friend. The atmosphere in the class should be conducive to learning. Teaching is essentially a practical skill, and it is felt that teachers must transform themselves into best performers. Every new lecture in a sense is a new performance for every teacher. A teacher should not remain static behind the podium, but must walk between the rows, occasionally take a look at what students are writing, talk to students and give them a pat on their back or give them compliments. Even such simple actions can create wonders in a large class as by doing so, a teacher adds his or her personal touch to every class. For successful teaching and learning, a sense of camaraderie must be established between the teacher and the student.

Learner-Centred Classes

It is true that it is difficult for a teacher to remember names of all students in large classes. However, it is felt that a teacher should make an attempt to remember names of the maximum number of students. If the teacher addresses students by their names, a bond is established between a teacher and a student and students feel 'special' and involved. A well-known essayist G.K. Chesterton has rightly said, 'The really great man is the man who makes every man feel great'. Making our classes learner-centred is a need of the hour as this would motivate students to participate in several activities conducted by the teacher and ensure better learning that would eventually result into lifelong learning. The following are some suggestions for enriching students' linguistic and literary competence in large classes.

While teaching grammar, it is necessary that teachers give an opportunity to the students to see grammar working in context. In the teaching of grammar, rather than giving readymade rules to the students all the time, an inductive approach can be followed. For example, while teaching the present continuous tense, five sentences can be written on the blackboard and students can be asked to identify the common pattern in all these sentences. In other words, it is necessary to channelise the students' mind rather than giving them readymade rules. Once the students develop trust and confidence that their teacher is not going to be angry with them or scold them even if their answers go wrong, students start coming out of their shell . Some times while teaching the past continuous tense, I divide the class into ten groups, and ask each group to visit a different location in college, for example, the administrative office of the college, the playground, the parking, the staff-room and the canteen. Every group is given ten minutes to visit the spot and using the past continuous tense to report on return whatever they had seen. An activity of this kind helps the students in assimilating the functional features of the past continuous tense. Some students of the class have made very interesting observations. Such as, one of the students, 'Joseph was sleeping on his accountancy textbook in the library' while another said, 'Prof. Gupta was asking his wife on the phone to prepare pizza in the evening'. Sentences of this kind create moments of laughter in the class, and learning grammar no longer seems to be a monotonous activity for the students, on the other hand, it becomes a matter of fun and enjoyment. *It is important that teachers and students laugh together as this kind of sharing can play a very significant role in transforming the classroom into a centre of edutainment.* I have observed that students enjoy this activity a lot, and apart from testing their grammatical skill, many hidden talents and capabilities of the students are revealed through this activity. While teaching indirect speech, a humorous conversation on television can be shown to the students and they can be asked to put that conversation into indirect speech.

Activity 1

Enriching vocabulary is an essential aspect of language teaching. Several activities can be conducted in the class in order to enhance students' word power. For example, I once divided one of my classes with a strength of a hundred students into ten groups and showed them a report of the film 'Slum Dog Millionaire' on the OHP. Twenty words from this report were underlined. Each group was asked to substitute the underlined words with near-synonyms. Students were allowed to make use of a dictionary and it was announced at the beginning of this activity that the group that would get the maximum correct answers in fifteen minutes would get a small prize. The students participated in this activity with a healthy competitive spirit and were deeply involved in the task assigned to them. The advantage was that the entire class was engaged in playing with words and discussing the words. As a result, there was a lot of peer learning as attempts were made to guess the meaning of the words from the context. As groups referred to the dictionary, even the weak students in the class lost their inhibitions and started communicating with their peers. Thus, it is felt that well set-up tasks, with clear instructions can be carried out with planning even in large classrooms.

Activity 2

Occasionally, I divide the class into groups and ask every group to write words that are normally used in a news report on murder or in other news items. An activity of this kind gives a lot of scope to the students to interact, argue and explain. Therefore, conducting such activities is a rewarding experience both for the teacher and the students. It is felt that the teacher should think of several creative activities, form the groups and write the names of students of every group on the notice board one day before the class, in order to save time and thereby set the whole class in action.

Activity 3

One of the activities that I often conduct in my classes is to give students a string of words (for example, waterfall, mobile, satisfaction, house, suicide, school and quarrel), and ask every group to write a story about a page long making use of these words. It turns out to be an interesting exercise, as every group has a different perspective and comes out with a novel idea in their story. In just an hour, students get a chance to listen to sad, happy and humorous stories and also stories full of suspense. An activity of this kind helps to enrich students' creative abilities, imaginative power, writing skill, and above all their ability to socialize and work with others in the group.

It is necessary to remember that while conducting such activities, the teacher's role is crucial. Like a north star the teacher should constantly be present in the class and guide the students, but at the same time allow the learners to take the centre stage and get them involved in various activities. The teachers' information, body language, immediate feedback and his or her very presence can play a pivotal role in transforming the classroom into a centre of good learning.

Teaching Literature in Large Classes

Literature is open to multiple interpretations and even in large classes there is a lot of scope for a teacher to initiate discussions. Before reading the text, the teacher can ask some pre-reading questions to the students in order to prepare them for the theme of the text. It is essential *to* connect the text with students' life while dealing with a literary text. Let me narrate one of my personal experiences of dealing with the poem 'The Road not Taken' written by Robert Frost.

Before commencing the class, one of my students told me that that was going to be her last lecture as she had decided to leave the college due to several problems in her life. I felt sorry for her and asked her to meet me after the lecture. When I started teaching the poem, I asked them some pre-reading questions. For example, 'Do you like to take challenges in life?' and 'What kind of major problems have you faced in your life so far? Several students made an attempt to answer these questions and the various responses given by students made the student realise the fact that problems are a part of everyone's life. She also understood that some other students had greater problems than what she was going through.

While making a line to line analysis of the poem, students were given an opportunity to ask questions, guess the meanings of the words from the context of the poem and discuss various aspects of the poem. The stimulating discussions in the class helped the students to comprehend and enjoy the poem. There was a lot of discussion on the last two lines of the poem, 'I took the one less travelled by, /And that has made all the difference'.

These lines motivated the student to accept all the challenges and continue her education in spite of all her problems. As a teacher, I was happy to see the fighting spirit that was developed in the student after studying this poem. It is felt that every teacher must encourage students to see the connection between life and literature, as this can help students to live a better life. It must always be remembered that one of the aims of teaching literature is to make our students better human beings.

The literary texts in the syllabus should be used as resources for stimulating discussion in the classroom. If several students are given an opportunity to voice their ideas and feelings, sometimes a teacher gets a new perspective from the students and this can prove to be a learning experience for the teacher as well. Since literature is multi-dimensional, a teacher must always be ready to think and accept new interpretations given by the students and appreciate their creative responses. Occasionally, group discussions can be conducted which can help to trigger the students' interest. The activity of role playing can be conducted in the class through which students can practise using language in different day-to-day situations. In all these activities, the teacher's role is important as the teacher has to prompt the students and provide valuable feedback and suggestions at different junctures.

Paying Personal Attention to Students in Large Classes

It is necessary for the teacher to give some extra time to the students beyond the regular lecture schedule. The teacher can make manageable groups of students and meet every group at least once in a month. During this meeting, the teacher can provide feedback to the students on their written assignment, make some suggestions and clear their doubts.

This kind of informal conversation enables the teacher to know every student individually, and it helps to strengthen the relationship between the teacher and the students.

Generally, in our educational system the teacher reads whatever the students write only after the term-end examination and the final examination. Since in most cases, the answer scripts are not shown to students after these examinations, sharing the answer would be a highly rewarding activity as it would help students to understand their shortcomings, and the teacher can give them a direction for improvement. One of the major advantages of this exercise is that every student is able to establish a dialogue with the teacher. An activity of this kind demands a lot of hard work, additional time, planning and patience on the part of a teacher. However, since it is likely to lead to a better kind of learning, it is felt that every teacher must possess a desire to teach the students even beyond the classroom hours. It has been observed that in such meetings, the weak and shy students feel comfortable. They feel happy when they receive compliments from their teacher and gradually they start participating with a lot of enthusiasm even in large classes.

It is generally believed that the learner-centred approach cannot be adopted in large classes. It is hoped that the various activities discussed in this article would help every teacher to realise the fact that adopting the learner-centred approach is not only possible, but highly desirable. Since large classes are inevitable, we, as teachers, should not look upon large classes as difficulties but as *resources* and try to be innovative and creative even within the existing working conditions.

Since teaching is essentially a practical skill which is constantly evolving in nature, let us hope that every teacher of English in India would think of more creative activities to face the challenge of handling large classes in an effective manner so that language learning would prove to be a rich experience for the students and the teachers. It is necessary for us, as teachers, to employ good strategies adopted in the 'Tradition' of teaching English in India, and at the same time use our 'Individual Talent' so that we would be able to prepare our students to meet several challenges of today's competitive age.

14 Using a Dictionary

Shridhar B. Gokhale

Introduction

One of the most useful reference books that a student must be able to use efficiently is a dictionary. Training in the use of a dictionary needs to be imparted at the school level. However, if this is not done at the school level for some reason, it needs to be done at the undergraduate level. The use of a dictionary helps a student to be independent in his studies and offers him valuable information about various aspects of language use. Some teachers are in the habit of giving students meanings of all difficult words. Instead, they should make students refer to the dictionary and find out meanings of at least a few of the words on their own. Dictionaries are, in fact, best friends for anyone who wishes to develop one's competence in the use of a language.

The Frequency of Referring to a Dictionary

Teachers have perpetuated a few myths about the use of a dictionary. An important myth is that a student must refer to a dictionary as soon as he comes across a difficult or unknown word. In fact, this may turn out to be counter-productive. If a student has ten difficult words on a printed page, he/she will take an inordinately long time to read and comprehend the page. Finding out the meaning of each word appropriate to the context and then understanding the page is a frustrating and time-consuming experience. Students who try to follow the piece of advice given above are often found to be deficient in the skill of reading.

It must be understood that every word in a language is not equally important. Some words are more useful in our lives than some other words. The relative importance of a word often depends on factors like frequency and contextual spread of a word. We must know very well the words that need to be part of our active vocabulary, but it is all right even if we do not know everything about a word that deserves to be a part of our passive vocabulary. In case of a word from the active vocabulary, we need to know its meanings, but in case of a word from the passive vocabulary, we should be able to guess its meaning from the context. Of course, a student needs to look up all the important words in a dictionary. For example, if he is not sure about some word in the title of the passage or if he does not know a word which is often repeated in the text, he needs to check it in a dictionary. A student must develop the ability to distinguish between relatively important words and relatively unimportant words.

Some teachers advise their students to look up five or ten words from the dictionary every day and learn them by heart. Such an activity is never successful, firstly because it treats all the words in a language as equally important and secondly, it is not very useful to mechanically learn a list of words. Besides, there must be a strong reason to learn and remember a particular word. In other words, there must be a communicative need which is likely to be fulfilled by the learning of a word.

Monolingual and Bilingual Dictionaries

Most students, particularly at the elementary level, use bilingual dictionaries. The two languages in this case are English, the target language and the mother tongue, the source language. Such dictionaries satisfy students at the cognitive level, but they are not very effective in enabling a student to improve his competence in the target language. At higher academic levels, such dictionaries prove to be ineffective, because they often do not give all the words required at those levels nor do they give a large number of meanings of each of the words.

At the high school level, and certainly at the undergraduate level, it is necessary to encourage students to use a good monolingual dictionary i.e. an English–English dictionary. Generally such dictionaries give us more useful and plentiful information than bilingual dictionaries. Naturally they provide greater exposure to English to students, because when the latter check meanings, they read English. There are many dictionaries available now that endeavour to explain meanings in very simple English. For example, the *Longman Dictionary of Contemporary English* uses a defining vocabulary of only about 2000 words, i.e. all the meanings are given using only the words from this list. As a result, words used for giving explanations are easier than words being explained.

Pronunciation in Dictionaries

An important piece of information that each dictionary gives us is the pronunciation of a word. The pronunciation is indicated using the phonemic transcription. There are 44 phonemes or basic sounds in British English. Some of the phonemic symbols are the same as letters used in ordinary writing and students would easily understand the sounds represented by them. Any good dictionary provides the table of all the symbols with examples and it is possible for any intelligent person to learn the symbols in a relatively short span of time. Teachers too should learn the symbols and teach pronunciation using phonemic symbols.

Perhaps the most important aspect of pronunciation is accent or stress. In every good dictionary, accent is indicated by a short vertical stroke before the accented syllable. It has been proved that correct accentuation is more important than correct articulation of vowels and consonants as far as intelligibility is concerned. The teacher needs to make sure that in his own speech he makes the accented syllable most prominent.

Grammatical Information

A good dictionary offers valuable grammatical information. All dictionaries specify the part of speech of each word and give us more details about sub-categorization. For example, they specify whether a particular noun is countable or uncountable, whether a particular verb is transitive or intransitive and whether a particular adjective is gradable or non-gradable. Of course, teachers must be able to understand such categories and sub-categories and also know how to use these indirectly in the teaching of English. For example, a teacher must know that only a countable noun can be preceded by the indefinite article 'a' or 'an' and that only a countable noun has a plural form. He must know that a transitive verb needs to be followed by an object and that only a gradable adjective can be preceded by an intensifier. Every dictionary provides a list of grammatical symbols used in the dictionary and both teachers and students should be familiar with the symbols.

The most valuable grammatical information is provided by usage given in the dictionary. Usage refers to the actual way in which a particular word is used by the native users of the language. It is reflected in three or four sentences given after the meaning of each word. These days dictionaries generally offer us authentic examples under usage, that is, the examples are real-life sentences selected from the vast corpus collected using computers. Many times dictionaries offer us grammatical information which may not be found even in a grammar book. For example, if we wish to find out which prepositions can be used after the word 'different', we may not get this information from a grammar book. However, the usage given in the dictionary would definitely provide us with necessary information.

Meanings in Dictionaries

The basic function of a dictionary is to offer meanings of words. It may be noted that most words in English have two or more meanings and that the meaning might change according to the context in which the word is used. It is rather difficult to find out words having just single meanings. If a word has a large number of meanings, sometimes it is difficult to identify the meaning most relevant to the context. Some dictionaries indicate broad areas of meaning in such cases so that a reader can easily identify the required meaning. For example, the word 'earth' has a large number of meanings. The broad areas of its meaning indicated in the *Longman Dictionary of Contemporary English* are world, soil, land, to connect a piece of electrical apparatus to the ground, and animal's home. Many times it is not clear from the meanings of a word how it is used in the language. Study of usage helps us in such cases.

Collocation is a very important aspect of the use of a word. It refers to the use of a particular word only in the company of certain other words. For example, the verb 'do' collocates with the noun 'duty', but the verb 'make' does not collocate with it. Therefore, we can say 'do one's duty', but not 'make one's duty'. The adjective 'high' collocates with the noun 'standard', but not the adjective 'tall'. Therefore, we can say 'high standard', but not 'tall standard'. Dictionaries offer us valuable information about collocations. Another way of getting more information about collocations is to carefully study the usage of a word.

Most dictionaries offer us synonyms, antonyms and related words and they are very useful in enriching our vocabulary. Dictionaries also use various labels to give us more information about words. For example, variety labels like British English and American English, register labels like religious, scientific and legal, style labels like formal and informal, usage labels like taboo and labels like formal and informal, usage labels like taboo and archaic. All these labels provide us with valuable guidance in the use and non-use of these words in particular situations and contexts. Students must be advised to refer to these labels whenever they check a word in a dictionary.

Concluding Remarks

Each dictionary has its own peculiarity and an efficient user of a dictionary must spend some time familiarizing himself/herself with different types of information available in a dictionary. All such information is usually a part of the Introduction or Preface printed at the beginning of the dictionary. These days many dictionaries provide information about the relative frequency of a word in the language. This is based on the statistical analysis of the use of words in large corpora and gives an indication to teachers regarding the relative importance of a word in a language so that it can be appropriately made a part of students' active or passive vocabulary according to their proficiency and needs. Teachers must highlight the point that students need to make dictionaries their best friends and use them as much as possible. This will directly lead to enhancement of their linguistic competence. Both teachers and students need to refer to a good dictionary, whenever they have any doubt about the use of a word. Not only this, they also need to refer to it even when there is no doubt!

15 Remedial English: A Case Study[1]

Viney Kirpal

Particularly when one's students are adult learners from a socially disadvantaged background the teacher must try to teach them in as creative and empathic a way as possible. Only then will the students learn or feel deeply interested in the subject. It is true that teaching 'remedial' English in a manner that is exciting for the learners would doubtlessly increase the teacher's work but that is the only way in which the learners can be involved to make rapid progress.

The Remedial English course is given to those students who have formally learnt English for some years but need to unlearn some wrongly imbibed rules of the language and learn correct ones. It is always a challenge to offer it in a meaningful way to the students.

How Children Differ from Adult learners of Language

Teaching language to young children is a comparatively easier task. For one, the art of teaching has undergone systematic development so that highly specialized techniques are available to the teacher of a children's language class. Secondly, little children have pliable brain cells and can acquire three to four languages simultaneously without fear of interference of one language with another. Thirdly, the imitative tendency of children can be fully exploited and language learning made into a sort of game. Children, for instance, enjoy mimicking sounds and words that their teachers or parents have articulated in their presence. They are happy to chant alphabets in sing-song unison, to recite nursery rhymes and to sing songs, when playing games in class or outside. Thus, as they participate in so much imitative, rhyme-based language-cum-play activity, they go on acquiring certain basic structures of the language and internalizing them without experiencing any burden.

On the other hand, language teaching to adults is a very difficult task. Adult learners shun repetitive and imitative models of language[2] work and question whatever does not satisfy their intellect or their curiosity. Adult language learners want to *think* when learning the language. A South Indian linguistics teacher of mine at the university disclosed to us that he could never learn Hindi despite having joined a Hindi language course for beginners. The reason was that at age thirty-five, he was asked, like a child, to imitate model sentences such as/ gai hamei du:dh deiti hae / (The cow gives us milk). "How could I enjoy doing that?" he exclaimed and added, "Naturally, I gave up learning Hindi; I couldn't have gone on with those endlessly boring classes!" If a slight miscalculation on his teacher's part to give the student material that did not suit the learner's age could demotivate him, how much more delicate would be the mental state and response of the student of remedial English who has very little motivation and many more problems in re-learning a language?

Few teachers pause to acquaint themselves with the requirements of the remedial English learner. The fact that the student knows English, even if he or she knows it inadequately, is generally overlooked and hardly any effort is made to give him or her the material that would appeal to his intellect or level . On the whole, it would be no exaggeration to say that little or no attention is paid to such students to get them interested in language work. Thus, much teaching effort in remedial courses goes wasted.

Teachers – I mean even the well-meaning ones – are often faced with the dilemma of how to teach remedial English in an interesting way. They may be familiar with the different techniques of teaching remedial English but are unable to put the material across to the students in an arresting manner thus making the course a very dull matter. This need not happen. In this chapter, I shall try to show with the help of some exercises that it is possible to have some very stimulating and successful classes even in remedial English work[2]. Before I set about presenting the exercises I would like to give my readers some idea of the kind of students I have tried out the above-mentioned material with.

Case Study

My students were Scheduled Caste and Scheduled Tribe (SC/ST) boys and girls admitted into the Indian Institute of Technology, Bombay, between 1974 – 1997. In a diagnostic test taken by them, soon after entry, they were found to be extremely deficient in English. So a year long Special Course in English was designed for their training before they could be registered for the B. Tech. programme. In a couple of odd years, the group's composition may have changed a little towards a mix of urban, richer students and low income students but by and large the students of the Special Course were from a village background. Aged between 18 and 21, unlike the general category students they were a shy and inhibited group, firstly because they came from a certain background that has known and seen suppression for generations and secondly, because they had come into the IIT through affirmative action while the other students (the large majority, belonging to the high castes) had entered the IIT on merit through a highly competitive Joint Entrance Examination (JEE) and were very proud of their achievement. In Paulo Freire's words, learners from deprived backgrounds must "become more" than what they were[3]. He had experimented with adult literacy programmes in Brazilian slums and taught English to less privileged adults through passages built around their lives and history. The method is called 'conscientisation'. Much influenced by Freire's *Pedagogy of the Oppressed,* the English course instructors aimed at not only improving the language skills of the students but also at instilling greater confidence and self–belief in them and encouraging them to mix with the rest of the students. In keeping with these objectives the course concentrated equally on spoken and written English and the teaching time was divided between lectures, group work, individual presentations, speech practice in the language laboratory, role plays and group discussions. Out of class social interaction in faculty homes was also initially arranged to give them a feeling of belonging but unfortunately, it petered out as students stopped visiting the faculty after a few weeks, perhaps due to campus peer pressure to be independent.

The word 'education' comes from the Latin 'educare', which means to "draw out". To educate our students in the true sense of the word, we must draw out the information from them rather than feed it to them. The old method of explaining a given passage or extract line by line is out, if not an insult to the mental age and intelligence of the learner. On the other hand, the dialectical method of posing questions and letting the students work out the answers seemed more suitable. The dialectical approach with the learner at the centre formed the pedagogical pivot of our Special English course[4] We devised a number of thought-provoking exercises for the students to re–learn the English language. Some of these have been described below.

The illustrative extract reproduced in this paper is short enough to match the length of the paper. All the exercises listed here were not based on this passage alone. These exercises were set to familiarize the students with grammatical items, vocabulary and ideas of social significance based on the passages that the class studied. In addition, we gave the students sufficient scope for the play of their imagination and let them have some fun while they learnt English. The passage, 'The Ideal Village' (quoted below) was taken from 'Re-building the Village'. It is an extract from Mahatma Gandhi's speech on the ideal village. Although written in 1937, the passage contains much that is relevant and contemporary even today because not enough has been done towards rural development. The purpose of the exercises was to enhance comprehension and ensure greater reinforcement of the items taught. The chosen passage and exercises are merely illustrative of the approach we used. Teachers can choose any passage and set any type of exercises that suit the interests, level and age of the students.

The Ideal Village

An ideal village will be so constructed as to lend itself to perfect sanitation. It will have cottages with sufficient light and ventilation built of materials obtainable within a radius of five miles of it. The cottages will have courtyards, enabling householders to plant vegetables for domestic use and to house their cattle. The lanes and streets will be free from all avoidable dirt. It will have wells according to its needs and accessible to all. It will have houses of worship for all, also a common meeting-place, a common land for grazing its cattle, a cooperative dairy, schools in which industrial education will be mainly imparted, and it will have panchayats for settling disputes. It will produce its own grains, vegetables and fruit and its own Khadi.

Given cooperation among the people almost the whole of the programme other than model cottages can be worked out at an expenditure within the means of the villagers without Government assistance. With that assistance there is no limit to the possibility of village re-construction. But my task just now is to discover what the villagers can do to help themselves if they have mutual cooperation and contribute voluntary labour for the common good. I am convinced, that they can, under intelligent guidance, double the village income as distinguished from individual income. There are in villages inexhaustible resources – for local purposes in almost every case. The greatest tragedy is the helplessness and unwillingness of the villagers to better their lot.

Exercise 1: We divided the class into groups of four and asked each group to divide the unknown words in the passage among themselves. Thereby, each group would get 3 to 4 words to work on. They were asked to first guess their meanings from the context and only later consult the dictionary to understand which of the meanings of a given word would suit the text under study. Once sure, they were to write down the word with an example to show its meaning in their notebooks. The exercise ended with the different groups presenting their work before the class. We made it a point to praise their work whenever we could.

Exercise 2: Students were paired up and asked to teach one another the meanings and spellings of the difficult words. I have found that peer teaching works wonders in teaching language to remedial learners as each student understands his fellow student's difficulties better than any teacher can. We used peer teaching to advantage with the comparatively more competent-in-English students helping the less competent ones. It instilled pride in both sides.

Exercise 3: In place of the conventional comprehension questions, we used some "visual" comprehension. We asked the students to read the passage carefully and make a drawing that would bring out the meaning of the passage. In this case, it was to draw the ideal village envisaged by Gandhi. It was not the quality of the drawing that mattered but the number of important details that the students remembered to put into the sketch. After their drawing was complete, the students could check up the missing items by looking at the passage again and add them to the drawing. This exercise aimed at comprehension in which no active linguistic effort was required. Of course, sketching was not possible with every passage for example, a passage with ideas of an abstract nature – but it was tried out wherever possible. It gave even those students the confidence who had understood the passage but did not know how to put across their points linguistically.

Exercise 4: Students were asked to read the passage carefully and mark all the key words which seemed important in conveying the ideas and thoughts expressed in the passage. The students were asked to join these words in short meaningful sentences. This gave them the central Idea of the passage. Teaching them this method gives students the confidence that they can write about what they have understood of the passage.

Exercise 5: Instead of spoon feeding students with grammar rules we used the passage to teach the students certain grammatical units such as the articles, and nouns (both countable and uncountable), by asking them to discover and frame the grammatical rules for themselves. For example, why was 'a' used in one line and 'the' in the next. This ensured that their attention was engaged and their understanding of grammar was more reason-oriented and hence more lasting.

Exercise 6: We asked them to write about the conditions that prevailed in the village or town to which they belonged. Next we asked them to record their ideas of an ideal Indian village or town today. This could be a group or individual effort, or a mixed exercise with discussions being held in the group and writing being done by the individual students. Whenever possible, we encouraged them to present their ideas to the class. This was an activity that the students liked. It also built up their confidence.

Exercise 7: Another exercise was to ask groups to fill in a crossword puzzle to check their knowledge of grammar or vocabulary already covered in previous classes. Occasionally we would also ask them to construct a crossword puzzle with the newly learnt words or grammatical items. It helped to make them learn new vocabulary and grammar in a joyous manner.

Exercise 8: A class discussion was sometimes arranged on the ideas in the passages. In this case the subject for discussion was 'The Importance of Cooperation'. We requested students to describe any activity in which they had participated in the recent past. We let as many pupils as volunteered to narrate their experience. Students came up with some very interesting answers. I shall mention some of these. A student described to the class how he helped build a school during the vacation in order to earn money for further studies; another spoke of having helped his father, and friends to build the village School Hall; a third told us of how, along with a friend, he taught youngsters in his village during his vacation, and a fourth described an experiment wherein he circulated his personal books among some children studying in the village School and was able to get them interested in the habit of reading. As students narrated their experiments in cooperation, the material for the topic of discussion became available to all the students.

Exercise 9: We also encouraged them to develop some dramatic activity or role play to enliven the class, besides giving students the confidence to express themselves in English. We divided the students into small groups and asked them to perform an act based on some idea related to the passage such as the panchayat deciding a serious dispute between two villages or something that would bring out certain customs or myths prevalent In the society to which they belonged. I remember some students playing the role of Ganesh, Parvati and Shiva to re-create the myth of why Ganesh has an elephant's trunk stuck on his face in place of a nose. In another class, we asked the students to choose their favourite TV advertisement and present it dramatically to the class in groups of four. They did very well and enjoyed themselves vastly. Role plays were useful in bringing out the introverted student who found that he, too, had something to talk about. It did not matter if our students used a non-English word or an incorrect expression here and there so long as they expressed themselves dramatically. We wanted them to overcome their shyness and that did happen.

Exercise 10: Getting the students to read a passage aloud was another exercise in confidence building and Spoken English skill development, which we tried out. The important point was to ask the students to read a paragraph slowly, alertly, in a loud and clear voice. The challenge was to be able to identify its main idea. Usually, this exercise was preceded by the whole class having first read the entire passage silently.

Exercise 11: Students were expected to listen to news on TV the previous night and summarize the main points in class the next day. We felt that this exercise would help them become more aware of world events and talk about them. Unfortunately, not all of them showed equal application perhaps because the TV was placed in the hostel common room and they couldn't switch on the news channel if other hostel inmates wanted to watch the second channel. Those were the days of Doordarshan TV with limited channels. But today, with some excellent documentaries available on Discovery, National Geography, Animal Planet, Fox, History & Entertainment, and Travel & Living channels, students can be asked to listen to good English on TV, Youtube or the internet and summarize the main points.

Exercise 12: We introduced students to the techniques of fast reading. Newspaper editorials provided convenient reading material. After some practice students were able to use their eye spans better and summarize the main idea of the passages. It was a near miraculous discovery to see some of these students being able to read at 600 words per minute and summarize the central idea of the piece correctly.

Exercise 13: We taught the students Public Speaking and made every student speak before the class for a couple of minutes. The more often they were made to come out and speak, the lesser was their diffidence each time. It is the one skill that rids students of stage fear and instill boldness in them. I believe that this is the one quality which helps less privileged students most because it improves, not only their speech content but also their body language and posture, universally regarded as marks of confidence. After having been silenced for so long, being encouraged to stand up before others and speak on different topics makes them feel mentally strengthened to take on a number of other challenges.

Exercise 14: If the batch was relatively better and had a few students who knew English more than the others, we introduced group discussion techniques to them and mixed the weaker with the better students. Here, we pushed the students further and made them speak and listen to one another. We taught them to take the argument forward and sum it up. All we did was to give them a structure for group discussion and monitored every student's performance closely on the spot, stopping them periodically to correct their direction, or letting them go on. Not all the students learnt to contribute evenly to the discussion, but it helped all of them and that was fine.

Conclusion: In all these exercises, the readers may please note that the role of the teacher was that of a facilitator. Our goal was mainly to stimulate and empower the students. Our focus was the learner whose language abilities and general confidence we wanted to see growing by the day. Socially disadvantaged, less privileged students are a part of every college now. Their composition may change from region to region or year to year, but the need to educate them with positive intervention remains a challenge. We may choose to ignore their presence and let the deserving poor flounder through the system, or as educators we may do our best to enhance their development. Perhaps, that way we may be able to give back to society in a small way. Language classes offer a great opportunity to do so. By taking care that students are trained in reading, writing, listening and speaking in every class we can help students use English with one another in as natural conditions as actual communication situations. That takes away the sting out of remedial English teaching. It also makes it enjoyable for both the teacher and the taught to participate in an activity which can never be called "routine".

Notes and References

1. This is a virtually re-written version of the article 'Teaching remedial English the creative way'. *The Journal of English Studies, November* 1977:543 – 560.
2. In most educational institutions in India, attendance is compulsory. Teachers should take pains to make their Language classes more and more lively so that their students love to come to class.
3. The basic philosophy which underlines Freire's educational system is that it is "man's vocation to *be* more, that is, than what he is at any given time or place." According to Freire there are no developed human beings except in the biological sense and so it is every person's endeavour to "transcend a given state." He believes that Education is not a neutral process. It can free an individual or it can "domesticate" him in a certain way. Education can recondition. Man alone has the capacity to know what conditions him and to reflect upon his actions. The key is in asking questions and encouraging a dialogue about the learner's reality. Summarized from Joao de Veiga Coutinho's Preface to Freire's, Paulo. 1970 *Cultural Action for Freedom*. Harmondsworth: Penguin Education, Penguin Books Ltd., 1975. Rev. edn: 8-9.
4. I am grateful to my former colleague Professor Dr. N. Talwar, who was Co-Instructor on the Special English course for introducing me to Freire's approach to language teaching.
5. 'Rebuilding the village' in *A Gandhi Anthology Book II*. Compiled by Desai, V.G. (1952) Navjivan Publishing House: 15-16.

16 The Testing of Language Skills

Shridhar B. Gokhale

Introduction

Unfortunately, there is a considerable degree of opaqueness about the testing of language and very often the marks awarded to a particular answer constitute a mystery for the student and even the teacher. The aim of this article is to enable teachers to enhance the degree of transparency in assessment and minimize the element of chance or luck in language testing.

The Teacher's Linguistic Competence

The most important factor that influences even a sincere teacher is his/her own linguistic competence. It is assumed that the teacher must have thorough knowledge of the subject that he teaches or assesses. In simple words, the teacher must know all the correct answers so that he can confidently mark answers right or wrong.

Multiple Correct Answers

One of the major problems here is the multiplicity of correct answers, particularly in the areas of pronunciation, grammar or vocabulary. The teacher may favour a particular correct answer for some reason, but he must be aware of the other possible answers. It is well-known that words like *direct, education, immediate* and *sixteen* have two correct pronunciations and before the teacher judges a particular pronunciation to be right or wrong, he/she must confirm all the correct answers by referring to a dictionary. In one of the workshops conducted for teachers, I asked practising teachers to fill in the blank in the following sentence by using a correct preposition. This approach is different —— other approaches. Most teachers chose the preposition 'from', which, is the correct answer. Some teachers chose in addition, either 'than' or 'to'. However, no teacher was aware of the fact that all the three prepositions mentioned above are perfectly acceptable. If the teachers were to assess students' answers to the same question, there would be a considerable degree of interpersonal variability and the same answer would be marked 'right' or 'wrong' by different teachers. The issue is made more difficult by the fact that the textbook prescribed may mention only one of these possibilities. In the workshop, I asked teachers to imagine that the textbook uses the preposition 'from' and then asked them how they would mark the answers 'than' and 'to'. One of the teachers promptly answered that the answer given in the textbook would receive one full mark, whereas the other correct answers would receive half a mark each. I asked him why he would do that. The answer was, 'One full mark for knowing the textbook and half a mark for not knowing the textbook, but knowing the correct answer'. I retorted by saying that those who gave the answer other than the one given in the textbook deserved more marks for knowing the language well. The point is that the examiner must not impose his prejudices and preferences on to students, and treat all correct answers fairly and justly.

Fairness to Students

This suggests that even if the teacher is sure about the answer he must check all possible answers by referring to the usage in the dictionary before he begins the assessment. In many universities and examination boards, model answers are prepared and handed over to examiners for ensuring uniformity of assessment. It is possible that the moderator or the person who prepares model answers does not foresee all the possible correct answers. The examiner faces a moral dilemma in such situations and it is difficult for him to decide what to do. If he follows the moderator, there will be uniformity of assessment among all the examiners, but he may be unjust to some of the students. If he follows his conscience and tries to do justice to all students, he disobeys the moderator and there is no uniformity of assessment. It is, indeed, difficult to decide what must be done in such a situation.

I would like to suggest that our loyalty as an examiner to the English language should be stronger than our loyalty to the moderator. I believe that fairness to students should be the supreme guiding principle in such cases. Of course, the examiner should contact the moderator at the earliest and discuss with him the multiple correct answers and persuade him to accept all correct answers. Of course, it is imperative in all such cases that the examiner is absolutely certain about what he suggests. When the examiner becomes a moderator later, he must ensure that all correct answers are specified.

It is obvious that we need to have teachers and examiners who have sound linguistic competence and who are conscientious and hard-working enough to ensure that academic injustice is never done to students.

It is necessary that the questions set and instructions contained in the question paper are absolutely clear and unambiguous and that all the examinees interpret them in the same way. The examiner should use verbs like 'discuss', 'explain', 'elaborate' and 'exemplify' very carefully and they must indicate to the examinees the task that is expected to be fulfilled. Most students do not pay much attention to the phrasing of the question and produce a roundabout stock answer which is not really relevant to the question. Task fulfillment must be considered an important aspect of the answer and it must be evaluated accordingly.

Clear and Unambiguous Questions and Instructions

It has been observed that sometimes examinees are asked to fill in the blanks in a given passage. The question should specify whether only one word is to be used for filling in each blank or whether a number of words are expected to be used for the purpose. Therefore, the question may be worded as:

Fill in the blanks in the following sentences, using only one word in each blank.

OR

Fill in the blanks in the following sentences using one or more words in each blank.

Global Marking Vs Componential Marking

Global Marking involves assigning a global mark or grade to an answer which is often very long and which is intended to reflect different skills at the same time. The mark is based on an overall impression created by the answer. It has been noticed that there is a lot of interpersonal variability in such marking. That is, there is a wide variation in the marks assigned to the same answer by two or more examiners. It has also been noticed that there is a considerable degree of intra-personal variability in such marking. That is, the same examiner may assign different marks to the same answer on two different occasions.

The problem can be solved to some extent by what is known as componential marking. In this the examiner thinks about different significant components of an answer and formally or informally assigns separate marks for each component. For example, if an essay-type long answer is assigned 25 marks, its different components may be thought to be content, planning and organization, cohesion and coherence, examples to illustrate main points, vocabulary and grammar etc. The examiner may assign maximum marks to each of these components. For example, he may decide that out of 25, he would assign 5 marks to content, 4 marks to cohesion and coherence, 6 marks to vocabulary and grammar etc. A particular student may get 3 marks out of 5 for content, 2 for cohesion and coherence, 3 for vocabulary and grammar etc. If these marks are totalled, the marks assigned to the answer are likely to be more objective and reliable. Componential marking may considerably reduce the problems of interpersonal and intrapersonal variability.

Concluding Remarks

Testing is often seen as a 'necessary evil'. Students hate it and many teachers consider it to be 'unwanted work'. However, it provides valuable feedback both to students and teachers. It is important that both the questions set by the teachers and the assessment are totally reliable and fair. The teacher must have sound linguistic competence and love for the students in order to achieve this objective.

English for Professional Purposes

17 Writing Emails
Viney Kirpal

At a Faculty Development Programme, a young lecturer of Computer Science was making a presentation on the technical aspects of sending and receiving emails when I casually asked him if he himself was a user of emails. His answer was 'No'. I was really surprised and said so. I told him that a teacher who teaches others how to use the email facility and does not know how to write it himself is a contradiction. Subsequently, I discovered that many teachers do not know how to use the email or write one well.

This is unfortunate because almost all our students use the email today. Teachers could as well learn how to use it to communicate with their students for announcing course assignments, grades, upcoming discussions, and other important information. Creating web courses, giving the outlines of lectures, providing lecture power point slides and video-recordings of the teacher's lectures, announcing assignments and deadlines are the order of the day in the west and in some of the more progressive educational institutions in India such as the IITs and IIMs. All this begins in first getting comfortable with writing and receiving emails, which in my view, is the simplest use of the computer.

Why Teach Email Writing

While the majority of students and a few teachers do use email communication they use it largely for informal interaction. This means they write emails the way they would speak with a friend using abbreviations and all. The need, however, is to know how to use it effectively in professional situations because business and education today are growing increasingly internet-centric. An educated person who cannot write good emails in the contemporary scene is considered akin to one who is illiterate. No business organization will tolerate a professional who cannot communicate suitably on email with customers and colleagues. Universities and colleges abroad make an extensive use of the email. The trend is catching up here, too.

Link up Email Writing with the Syllabus

As teachers of language, we can link up our syllabus requirements with the future linguistic needs of our students. This will also help students see the value of studying language in college. One of these value propositions obviously lies in learning how to write good business emails. Giving students extensive practice in the use of structure, writing good paragraphs, composing grammatically correct sentences -- activities that are usually taught in composition writing -- can easily build the base for teaching the students effective email writing. In fact, one may even go so far as to sometimes set them a question on email writing in place of essay writing and examine them for different aspects of language competence.

You might ask, 'Why do we need to learn how to write effective emails?' My answer is : We need to develop this skill because emails are a written form of communication which, if designed ineffectively, can cause misunderstandings and loss of time, customers and their goodwill, generate frustration or rouse anger in the receiver. Written communication is always more prone to negative interpretations than the oral because of the absence of facial expressions such as a smile or the soft tone which can offset an otherwise blunt verbal message. For example, a professional once wrote to a customer, 'I am busy and can't attend to your work just now'. The customer immediately called up his boss and asked him to take the employee off the project otherwise he would 'withdraw the project altogether' from the company. Losing a customer or his goodwill is not acceptable to organizations especially if it is triggered by an inappropriately constructed email message sent out by an employee.

To ensure such mishaps do not occur, organizations often hold costly workshops to train up employees in "Written Business Communication", which generally includes email writing. The language teacher can play a pragmatic role by providing this useful training in her class and developing her students for their future responsibility as writers of good business emails.

Essential Components

What should we teach when we train our students for business email writing? In my view, focusing on five essential components and giving our students adequate practice in each should enable them to write effective emails. The components that are basic to the composition of business emails are :

1. Format
2. Protocol
3. Structure of the email message
4. Netiquette
5. Clarity and correctness

Each is explained at length below so that the teacher can teach these components with greater confidence.

1. Format

A number of email users need to be made aware that while informal emails can be written in any manner, business email writers must use the proper format. Teachers need to train students in the appropriate format so that they can write effective emails.

Every email message uses the American letter format shown below. This means that every line starts along the left margin. This includes the salutation and the complimentary close. No space needs to be left after the margin to indicate the beginning of a new paragraph as is customary in the British letter format (also shown below). Every paragraph is typed in single spacing with a double space provided between two paragraphs to indicate a paragraph break.

British Letter Format	American Letter Format
Receiver's Address	Receiver's Address
Sender's Name Date	Sender's Name Date
Address	Address
Salutation	Salutation
Complimentary Close	Complimentary Close

In the American format, both the receiver's address and the writer's address are written on the left side next to the margin. So, in a way, this format is easier to remember than the British format, which is more popular in Indian universities but not in all business communication. Software companies, BPOs and other modern business houses use the American format. This point should be shared with the students because they may have noticed these variations in use. You may, if you have the time, begin by giving them a sample each of the American and the British letter formats and asking them to list their distinctive features. This will help the students learn and remember the two formats better because they will have interacted closely with them. Remember, at the end of the exercise to repeat that this was mainly to help them understand the distinct formats and their particular characteristics. **However, for writing emails, they must use only the American format.**

One of the most important features of the email format is the **Subject line**. The Subject line should be written very carefully. It should briefly communicate the essence of the sender's letter so that the receiver recognizes the significance of the email and reads it. In times when it is common for employees to receive 30 to 150 emails a day, the importance of crafting the Subject line with due effort cannot be over-emphasized.

2. Protocol

Closely linked with the format are the salutation and the complimentary close. Students and young professionals often think that it is all right to write 'Hi' without a name, or 'Hi All' or even not to use a salutation in an email. This may work with informal or semi-formal emails. For business emails, it is customary to begin with a formal greeting (such as Dear/Sir/Madam/Ms/ Mr.X) as in a business letter. A first time email communication will also carry the complete address and designation of the addressee on the top left corner of the email. The closure similar to the formal letter should include words such as Yours sincerely,/Yours faithfully, followed by the writer's complete name, designation and address on the bottom left corner of the email.

If, in reply, the recipient signs off with his or her first name, it is an indication, that we too may use our first name, and address the receiver's by their first name in future emails. If, however, the recipient prefers to use the formal salutation (Dear Mr. Rutherford/Ms. Nina Rutherford), then it is best to stay formal with the protocol when writing to them. American clients usually prefer the informal Hi/Hullo followed by their recipient's first name. They would also sign off with their first name. The British are trying to follow the Americans but sometimes they use the formal 'Dear Mr. Rutherford' and sign off informally as `John.' The Germans are quite conscious of their titles; so are the Japanese, though individual variations veering towards American protocol may be seen. The point to remember is that it is good to be aware of cultural preferences but the thumb rule is to follow the style used by the foreign sender or receiver of the email especially the one with whom we are doing business. While ending an email, it is customary to sign off with 'Best wishes' or `Best regards' followed by a comma and one's name, except for the first time when it is usual to sign off with Yours sincerely, / or Sincerely, followed by one's name and surname.

3. Structure in Emails

The third component is the Email structure. Like all writing, good email messages must also be designed using a certain framework. The simplest of these structures is given below :

Example

Salutation	Hi/Dear
Paragraph 1 Gives the main message in one or two lines.	I am writing to request you to send me the following items at the earliest.
Paragraph 2 Elaborates the message using details such as what, which, how, where, when. etc.	I need a new Pentium 4 with XP and a laser printer within the range of Rs. 35,000/- at my office address given below: _____ _____
Paragraph 3 Sums up the main message and desired action with a motivator for the recipient.	You have always been very prompt in sending me the goods I have needed. This time too I hope to get my new Pentium 4 and printer within two days.
Complimentary close	Thank you. Best regards, Anand Srivastava

The second structure is a variant of the first. It is the one we may use to send a complaint. The framework follows:

		Example 1	Example 2
Salutation		Dear Sir:	Hi Rajesh:
Paragraph 1 States the complaint briefly in a line or two		This is to inform you that the fridge that I have bought from you is defective.	Thank you for your email providing the codes for the requested software.
Paragraph 2 Provides more details		I had bought it from you vide invoice no.——— dated ———	We had been waiting for your proposed software with much anticipation but unfortunately the software did not work on our customer's machines.
Paragraphs 3 & 4 Briefly state the causes and the consequences of the defect/complaint		Unfortunately, the thermostat is defective and the fridge is not cooling.	
		This has caused a great deal of inconvenience to me and my family.	We would have expected you to test your software before sending it to us.
		Consequently, we are experiencing much inconvenience as I am not able to use the fridge.	This incident has caused us great embarrassment as our customer has openly expressed his annoyance to us.
Paragraph 5 Sums up desired action and by when expected		Yours is a reputed company and I have bought your product in good faith. I expect you to repair or exchange my fridge immediately.	Please let me know why this has happened and by when the problem can be resolved to our satisfaction.
Complimentary Close			

4. Netiquette

You will notice that in all the structures provided in this paper so far, the emphasis is on courteous but firm communication. The sender motivates the recipient to respond to his/her request for action either through an expression of trust or through assertion. Under no circumstances should impolite or offensive language be used. The aim of all business communication is to build or retain goodwill and get the desired action. This is what is meant by Netiquette. Entire websites are devoted to teaching people Net manners because they are so important in formal emails. A few email manners are mentioned below.

It is considered bad manners to call people names, to use slang or become aggressive in email messages. Just as in verbal communication, one is expected to maintain decorum no matter what the provocation, so it is with written business communication. Perhaps more so, because interpretations of the written message can vary depending on our mood or relationship with the sender. Generally, Indians are more prone to becoming emotional and reacting with defensiveness or belligerence. They tend to respond with angry words and use capital letters and exclamation marks to express their feelings of annoyance, exasperation or injury. These are regarded equivalent to abusing and shouting and not tolerated in professional circles. Consider example 2 of the structure of complaint email given above where a foreign client has expressed his displeasure with the defective software code sent by the Indian developer working on his project. The developer is more likely to explode in words than to give a well-reasoned reply. But netiquette states very explicitly that the sender must not scream at his or her recipient nor show anger in their emails. Even when the receiver has received a disturbing email, one is expected to answer only in a rational, firm and solution–oriented manner.

The two contrasting sample email replies with their structures might read as follows:

Sample 1

Structure	Example of Email reflecting Bad Net Manners
Salutation	Hi John:
↓	
Expression of anger	I am SHOCKED at your ACCUSATIONS! Of course I had checked the software on my machine before sending it to you. I don't work shabbily; you KNOW that I think by now. If not, then let me tell you how misunderstood and hurt I have felt with your email!
↓	
Defensive explanation	
↓	
Violent emotional reaction, unmindful of its impact on one's relationship with the sender.	My team and I sat in office until midnight the whole of last week to complete and test the software so that you could demonstrate it to your customer. We are feeling very demotivated.

With warm regards,
Sharan

Sample 2

Example of Email written Politely but Firmly

Structure	
Salutation	
Expression of regret.	
Possible causes of problem.	
Proposed solution	
Expression of concern and lasting good will.	

Hi John:

I am sorry to know that the software did not work on your customer's machine. I can understand the embarrassment it must have caused you. We had tested it twice on our machines and also on Roger's machine in your office. The software had worked well both times.

Is it possible that your customer's machines are not compatible with yours and ours?

Could you please check the software on your machine and demonstrate it to the customer on it?

If we get some more details of your customer's machine, we can further customize the software for his use.

Please let me know soon of your experience of testing the software on your machines. We value you as a customer and will always strive to give you our best.

Best regards,
Sharan.

As you can see, Sample 2 is definitely superior to Sample 1 and also more conducive to preserving customer goodwill and cordial relationships. An employee who is capable of retaining a company's customers especially with his written communication is considered an asset while one who loses them is shown the door at the earliest. It is a well-known fact that acquiring a new customer costs five times more than keeping an old one and no company would like their employee to cause them a loss of customers. The teacher of English can groom her students to learn the art of polite, assertive, helpful written business communication so that it becomes ingrained in their character and personality even before they take up a profession. Writing emails that are courteous and devoid of exasperation or indignation is universally considered good manners.

Other Do's and Don'ts

Using SMS language and abbreviations such as asap (as soon as possible) is acceptable only in cell phone messages or informal emails but is regarded as bad manners in business emails. Some email writers think that using short forms such as 'u' for 'you' and '2' and '4' instead of 'to' and 'for' show cleverness and smartness. They need to be told that such email writers are looked down upon as people who are unaware of the prevailing etiquette. It is important to correct them in proper time. Netiquette also includes using polite words such as 'please' when making a request, 'sorry' as an expression of regret and 'thank you' as a mark of gratitude for help rendered. Indians often feel that the use of such words is artificial. But worldwide the culture of courteous communication - written and oral - expects these expressions of politeness and we must not make up for our ignorance of good manners by rationalizing it. On the contrary, blunt communication is regarded as downright rude. If we were to examine the business communication we receive from our western clients we would both be surprised and impressed with the courteous and humble manner in which they communicate. We could learn a lot from them.

Answering an email or acknowledging one within 24 hours is considered polite. This point needs to be impressed upon students. We often believe that not to acknowledge an email or not to send a timely reply is alright specially when we wish to decline a request. We also think that the sender 'will understand' that we have received their email. However, etiquette demands that we send in a polite regret or acknowledgement and not keep people guessing.

Again, many of us believe that not to proofread our emails or check our spellings and punctuation is fine in electronic communication. In reality these lapses are regarded as poor communication manners. With the facility of spell check available on every computer this activity would take us just a few seconds. Similarly, proofreading our emails would create a better image of us than when we send out emails replete with mistakes. It is also good manners to use the same font and font size throughout the email. Font Arial is recommended and the preferred size is font 10 for emails. The use of colours is to be avoided unless writing to someone with whom we have a semi-formal relationship. For business emails, the black coloured font is best. Above all, uniformity of font and size is considered appropriate. Emails where different fonts and font sizes are used have been considered untidy and shabby.

5. Clarity and Correctness

This brings us to the last component of effective email writing, namely clarity and correctness. Spending a few minutes to clarify the purpose of writing an email helps in designing precise messages. This includes asking ourselves the question whether or not we need to write the email at all, or will a phone call or face– to–face meeting serve the purpose better.

A common complaint of foreign clients is that our professionals write lengthy, verbose, unclear emails. Long-winded emails waste a receiver's time and discourage them from reading or answering them. This is an aspect that needs to be ingrained in our students through repetition and practice. Many write as if they were thinking aloud. This results in emails that are one or two page-long paragraphs whose meaning could be anybody's guess.

As I mentioned earlier, by linking email writing to the basic elements of continuous writing such as structure, proper paragraph writing and grammatically correct sentences, we can train our students to write clear and purposeful emails. By insisting that students first identify their main message and put it down in the opening paragraph of their email, teachers can actually help students to think and write more concisely. It is when our ideas or our message is unclear that our emails become fuzzy. The quality of our writing mirrors the clarity of our thoughts. The more clear we are about what we want to convey, the more lucid will be our written communication, and vice versa.

Further, teachers may emphasize upon students the need to write their message in paragraphs numbered 1, 2, 3 etc. This helps clarity. Again, the paragraphs in the email must follow the usual principles of good paragraph writing, i.e. have a clear topic sentence, supported by appropriate details. This is the easiest way to construct clear emails. Clarity can be enhanced by writing simple sentences that are more grammatically correct than relying on complex and compound constructions.

Lastly, using the different email structures provided earlier in this article would ensure that one's emails are coherent as well as precise.

Correctness in Emails

Besides clarity, **correctness** in emails is also to be impressed on students. Correctness means more than correct spellings and punctuation. It means verifying and ensuring that the information that is provided in an email is correct. It means taking the pains to understand others' emails correctly and providing them with the information they want, preferably point wise. It means checking that every attached document and graphic is the correct one and that all the documents and graphics listed in the email have actually been attached. Lastly, correctness also means that the email is addressed to the right person so that it can be acted upon to our satisfaction.

To conclude, the five components of email writing, namely, format, protocol, structure, netiquette, clarity and correctness, if taught, and practised with rigor could fill up a whole semester. But once learnt, the skill of effective email writing could turn a student into an asset for his future employers.

With so many points to take care of while constructing an effective email message, it is obvious that the training for professional communication must begin early. Indisputably, the college English language class is the best place to begin this exercise.

Conclusion

18 English for Specific Purposes

Grace Jacob

In situations across the globe where English is taught as a subject for a number of years at school from primary to secondary and tertiary levels as a second or even a third language, the aim is to equip learners with a basic knowledge of the language in terms of grammar, vocabulary, reading and writing. In some schools the teaching of speaking and listening skills may also be included. The curriculum is designed keeping broad or general aims for teaching and learning English. Once learners graduate and enter areas of study or occupation, they are expected to apply their knowledge of English to the contexts in which they are placed. These contexts may be academic or occupational. The teaching of English in these contexts of higher education is combined with the specific area of study or occupation that learners choose. The term English for Specific Purposes (ESP) is used to describe teaching and learning programmes which aim at equipping learners with language skills for their study or work situations. These situations provide the immediate context for English language education.

Approaches to ESP

It was in the 1960s that ESP courses and materials first began to appear. One of the early attempts was 'A Course in Basic Scientific English' by J.R. Ewer and G. Lattore

---

Grace Jacob is a Ph. D. from CIEFL Hyderabad. She was a postdoctoral fellow at the University of Pennsylvania, USA. She has taught at Pune University and at the University of Ibb (Yemen). Currently, she is a Consultant for various organizations and research advisor with Pune University.

in 1969. They based their work on the notion of 'register' or the idea that language variations are manifested in linguistic properties of grammatical structure and vocabulary. Specific sentence patterns and vocabulary items that occurred in scientific English were identified and exercises were provided for practicing these structural and lexical items. Pedagogically, courses such as those developed by Ewer and Lattore were informed by structural linguistics.

During the 1970s there was a new orientation to linguistics with the notion of "communicative competence" (Hymes 1972) and language pedagogy received a fresh impetus. A new way of ordering the language syllabus in terms of communicative needs, functions, skills and processes was advocated (See Wilkins 1976, Widdowson 1978, Brumfit 1984 and others). It was maintained that an effective language syllabus is one that is directly related to the specific and limited academic or non-academic functions to which the learner might put the language. Thus ESP became an umbrella term to include both English for Occupational Purposes and English For Academic Purposes. Early attempts at developing communicative competence in ESP were related to the comprehension and composition of written texts in specific fields of study, for example, science and technology (See Widdowson1978). The materials produced were generally based on a linguistic analysis of written texts in terms of textual/discourse functions, since a continuous text became the unit of linguistic analysis.

The notion of ESP has been growing in refinement over the years. A distinction between *language description* and *learning process* in language education began to be emphasized (See Widdowson 1983; Hutchinson and Waters 1987). It was argued that while language descriptions are important for designing the content of the *syllabus* in terms of language items and topics to be included, the specification of both the *target situation* and *teaching methodology* are vital to curriculum/course design. It was emphasized that a target situation needs to be perceived in terms of the kind of learners one is dealing with, i.e., their background, their existing level of proficiency in the language and the desired proficiency level to be achieved for the situations in which they are placed. When it comes to methodology, language learning and communication go hand in hand. It is important to ensure that the learner is able to engage with the language meaningfully for communicative purposes. Classroom tasks therefore have to trigger this process of engagement. Hence while designing an ESP course, it is important to devise tasks or procedures for the learner to use language accurately/ appropriately for accomplishing communicative acts or functions in specific situations. Further, learning outcomes and learning processes are closely monitored and assessed in ESP courses as part of the accountability that course designers and teachers and administrators are required to maintain. Thus we can see that over the years there has been a paradigm shift from a linguistic or structural approach to a communicative/procedural one.

Parameters of Course Design

Based on the foregoing discussion we can list the following essential parameters for ESP course design (a) Learner needs/ target situation analysis (b) Learning theory and teaching methodology (c) Target language description (d) Evaluation/assessment of learning outcomes.

Learner Needs /Target situation analysis

As mentioned earlier the learners we have in mind are adults who have already made their professional or occupational choices. They may be engaged in a study situation or a work situation. Learners' *needs* therefore have to be listed and then prioritized. For example in a study situation they will require English for their academic purposes of reading, writing, speaking and listening. It is possible that reading and writing skills are more important than the other two language skills. The levels of proficiency required for each of the skills will depend on the tasks learners are required to perform in the course of study. The gap between the level of proficiency required as a target and the existing level of proficiency for each learner can be determined/assessed using a reliable *test of English language proficiency*. The gap will vary for each learner and will indicate his/her need(s) for language development.

Beyond needs at the level of language proficiency, the needs of learners also include attitudes/motivation to learning and learning style preferences and even constraints to be overcome. For example, learners may lack confidence, be indifferent or even overconfident and these attitudes could affect his/her learning progress no matter how well developed the course might be. *Questionnaires* and *informal interviews* with students/ employees and subject teachers/managers could provide the necessary understanding of learners' social and psychological orientation to learning. Such learners could benefit from the social support that the tasks in the course provide. Activities such as *pair* and *group* work that are built into the course could have the potential of triggering positive attitudes to language learning. In some situations the use of the mother tongue for providing instructions could also be helpful. Other instruments include *text/input materials gathering, consultations* with learners, managers etc. The input materials will indicate the nature of the subject matter that the learner is required to be able to handle/use in the form of written or visual texts for study or work.

Hence learner needs as perceived in a target situation is the *base line data* which one needs to have before visualizing the course content in terms of language inputs to be provided and the methodology to be adopted. Tests, questionnaires and interviews are important instruments to be devised keeping the situation in mind and a check list for analyzing learner needs and the target situation could include the following questions among others.

Who are the learners?

Age/sex

What subject knowledge do they have?

Some background knowledge/no background knowledge

What is their attitude to doing a course in English?

Positive /negative/indifferent

Why are the learners taking the course?

Compulsory/optional

What is their learning background?

Traditional regional language schooling/English medium schooling/any other

What teaching - learning techniques are they used to?

Traditional lecture/task based activities/any other

Why is the language needed?

Study/ work/ training/ status/ promotion/any other

How will the language be used?

Speaking/writing/reading etc.

What is the medium to be used?

Telephone/face to face/electronic media

What is the type of text or discourse that will be used?

Academic texts/lectures/informal conversations/formal interviews/technical manuals/any other

Who will the learner use the language with?

Native/non-native/ lay people/experts/etc.

Where will the language be used?

Lecture hall/hotel/workshop/telephone/ meetings demonstrations/any other

When will the language be used?

Concurrently with the subject course/ subsequently/ in service

How often will the language be used?

Frequently/seldom/most of the time
(Adapted from Hutchinson and Waters 1987)

Learning Theory and Teaching Methodology

The *rationale* for a course and its syllabus rests on a learning theory and sometimes more than one learning theory. We have already seen how there has been a paradigm shift over the years between what is understood as the "structural" and "communicative approaches to ESP course design."

Underlying the structural approach is "behaviourism" as a psychological theory of learning. According to this theory, all learning is imitative and repetitive. Language learning is therefore perceived as a mechanical process of habit formation through repeated encounters with language items viz., language structures. Language drills and pattern practice are basic to language teaching that adheres to a behaviourist theory of language learning. ESP courses in the 1960's were developed along these lines. It is after the 60's that we see a shift from a mechanical to a cognitive language learning theory influenced by cognitive psychology. Learning came to be perceived as a process of concept formation through hypothesis testing. In language learning, it was theorized that learners arrive/ perceive the rules of grammar through trial and error and engagement with the language rather than through imitating correct *sentences*. The minimal unit for linguistic analysis stretched beyond the sentence to continuous and complete stretches of language or *texts* and the language functions they perform in specific social contexts. A text and the context for the production of texts in language performance has hence become crucial in language teaching under the "communicative approach", and it was observed that underlying every text is a communicative language function which is performed.

Course designers and teachers of ESP today cannot overlook this powerful development, however some amount of *remedial grammar* still appears in course books because learners expect it and teachers believe in its value. In other words the contemporary ESP course design though basically directed towards communication and learning processes is often eclectic, drawing on the best from language learning theories both current and dated earlier. However, what a course designer cannot overlook is that the syllabus and teaching methodology, are closely in step with learning processes and expected outcomes.

The syllabus for an ESP course contains a statement of *learning objectives* and a description of the *language inputs* to be provided in order to fulfill the objectives.

Target Language Description

Objectives are based on the information that the target situation provides in terms of what the learner needs the language for. *Learning objectives* are a specification of how the mind of the learner is expected to process the language in performance The content/ materials in the *syllabus* are then developed keeping objectives in mind in terms of skills/language functions to be performed in a set of *tasks*. A task in this context is a problem solving activity which requires the learner to deploy language accurately/appropriately. Tasks are problem solving activities in that the learner is expected to close the gap in communication. For example, when a learner is asked to provide the missing words in a passage, he uses the context provided to make his choices. The items or materials that a syllabus provides are a break up of language for developing various abilities or skills and language inputs. A complete syllabus statement would hence indicate the break-up for different skills and sub-skills in terms of language items or texts for both *composition* i.e., oral and written and *comprehension* i.e. aural and visual/verbal. Both verbal and non verbal channels are included for developing the processes and skills of composition and comprehension.

General Learning Objective	Specific Learning Objectives	Language Inputs (Sample)
Conduct a conversation with a caller appropriately	Abilities:-open a conversation politely-make polite inquiries/ requests -provide information-use intonation appropriately, etc.	- Hello, this is the CIT, may I help you?- Could you hold on please?- I'm sorry, there is no response. Please try later, etc.

By way of an illustration let us imagine an ESP course that is being prepared to train telephone operators in a company. The course design entails charting out the General and Specific objectives and the language inputs to be provided as given in the table below.

Materials for such a course could be developed using different situations and the conversations could be with varying types of callers and inquiries. A list of questions are needed for identifying suitable materials to be presented in the form of **lessons or units**. Examples: *What are the different work situations to be listed? What are the language points to be covered? What kind of exercises/activities should be provided? What instructions should be provided for the teacher? What instructions should be provided for the learner?*

Assessing Learning Outcomes

ESP courses are essentially language proficiency courses that are specific to particular situations. *A proficiency test* administered at the end of the course will provide not only an assessment of learning outcomes but also important *feedback* to teachers and administrators.

The learning outcomes are expected to directly transfer to the work or academic situations. Implementation of the course therefore is a commitment to "deliver" in terms of successful training. Learners can be placed on a scale (1-5 or 1-9) to describe their levels of performance from limited to expert users. A cost effective test of proficiency will "produce" a fair number of *good users* of the language, a few *expert users* and some *modest users*. Explicit descriptors need to be provided for each of these levels of language proficiency. For example, a modest user has only partial knowledge of the language and is not able to communicate or process the language satisfactorily. A good user has a fair amount of command and an expert user is fully in command of the language (See Hutchinson and Waters, 1987, p.150). Feedback is useful to teachers and administrators for fine tuning the course before its next implementation. It has bearings both on the language inputs/materials provided and the teaching methodology.

Overview

At the outset I have underscored the fact that ESP courses today are essentially skills-based and designed for learners who have already had some background knowledge of the English language. ESP courses therefore attempt to develop language proficiency and provide specific context based language learning for occupational or academic purposes. When it comes to course design, it is possible to view historically two contrastive paradigms in terms of language learning theory and syllabus design and these have implications for the selection of language inputs/materials for triggering learning processes. Course designers could choose to be eclectic in their approach.

The starting point for ESP courses is a systematic needs analysis and target situation analysis. The findings direct the statement of objectives and selection of inputs to be provided for particular learners. Teaching methodology for a skills-based course is essentially task based and therefore the materials have to indicate this clearly to the learner and the teacher in order that tasks lead to desirable learning outcomes. Finally tests specially designed for particular courses will indicate proficiency levels and provide essential feedback to course designers, teachers and administrators

References

1. Brumfit, C (1984). *Communicative Methodology in Language Teaching. Cambridge:* Cambridge University Press.
2. Ewer, J.R and Lattore, G (1969). *A Course in Basic Scientific English.* London: Longman.
3. Hutchinson, T and Waters, A (1987). *English for Specific Purposes: A Learning Centred Approach.* Cambridge: Cambridge University Press.
4. Hymes, D (1972). On Communicative Competence' in *Sociolinguistics* Pride J.B. and Holmes, J. (eds). Harmondsworth: Penguin PP. 269-93.
5. Widdowson H.G. (1983). *Learning Purpose and Language Use.* London: Oxford University Press.
6. Widdowson, H.G. (1978). *Teaching Language as Communication.* London: Oxford University Press.
7. Wilkins, D.A. (1976). *Notional Syllabuses.* London: Oxford University Press.